PUNK: THE ILLUSTRATED HISTORY OF A MUSIC REVOLUTION / ADRIAN BOOT & CHRIS SALEWICZ

The Sex Pistols ...sponse brought joy to

ADRIAN BOOT & CHRIS SALEWIC

PUNK: THE ILLUSTRATED HISTORY OF A MUSIC REVOLUTION

PENGUIN
STUDIO

PENGUIN STUDIO
Published by the Penguin Group

Penguin Books USA Inc, 375 Hudson Street, New York, New York 10014, U.S.A.
Penguin Books Ltd, 27 Wrights Lane, London W8 5TZ, England
Penguin Books Australia Ltd, Ringwood, Victoria, Australia
Penguin Books Canada Ltd, 10 Alcorn Avenue, Toronto, Ontario, Canada M4V 3B2
Penguin Books (N.Z.) Ltd, 182-190 Wairau Road, Auckland 10, New Zealand

Penguin Books Ltd, Registered Offices:
Harmondsworth, Middlesex, England

First published in Great Britain by Boxtree Limited 1996
First published in the United States of America by Penguin Studio 1997

1 3 5 7 9 10 8 6 4 2

Photograph credits appear on page 158.

ISBN 0 14 02.6098 6

CIP data available

Designed by Stylorouge.
Printed in Great Britain. Set in Bureau grotesque.
The publisher wishes to thank Tim Stegall for his expert advice.

Luton Sixth Form College
Learning Resources Centre

"ANARCHY IN THE U.K"

BANNED IN THE U.K

ANARCHY IN THE U.K. Tour
SEX PISTOLS
FIRST MAJOR U.K TOUR WITH SPECIAL GUESTS
THE DAMNED
Johnny THUNDER'S HEARTBREAKERS
(Ex New York Dolls from USA)
THE CLASH
TOUR DATES
SINGLES AVAILABLE
℗ 1977 SEX PISTOLS

SEX PISTOLS
GOD SAVE THE QUEEN
ALL RIGHTS OF THE MANUFACTURER AND OF THE OWNER OF THE RECORDED WORK RESERVED UNAUTHORISED COPYING

INTRODUC TION : 8

CONTENTS

THE CLASH

intRODUCTION

When the Sex Pistols' mildly controversial television interview with the journalist Bill Grundy broke up in a barrage of four-letter words on 1 December 1976, the incident and its aftermath filled the front pages of Britain's tabloid press for an entire week. The media, it seemed, had gone mad; and so had other people too: an Essex lorry-driver was so infuriated by the group that he kicked in the screen of his television set.

This kind of response brought joy to the hearts of those who already understood that what was underway was a crucial and hilariously satirical cultural sea-change – and that within this battle against Babylon lay a metaphysical shift in the consciousness plates of humanity.

Certainly the exceptional and extraordinary events of this time marked a watershed not only in popular music or culture, but in attitudes and sensibility. In this overturning of the past, a new, more egalitarian world began to emerge: from now on, for example, rock stars – popular artists of

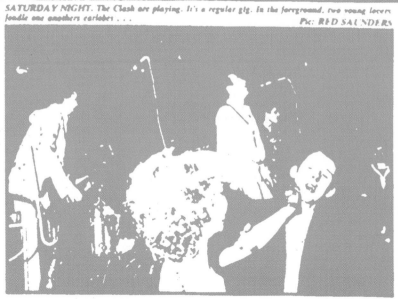

SATURDAY NIGHT. The Clash are playing. It's a regular gig. In the foreground, two young lovers fondle one another's earlobes . . .

Pic: RED SAUNDERS

CANNIBALISM AT CLASH GIG

(But why did they do it, MILES?)

any sort, in fact – were shown that it was unacceptable to behave with the dinosaur-like arrogance of erased consciousness that many such items had paraded since the 1960s. We really were leaving the twentieth century and entering a new time. Nothing would ever be the same again.

Punk was a new music, a stinging, relentless satire, an outrageously expressed scream for freedom that only expressed its depth of desperation. For it was also a necessarily harsh commentary on a hopeless, pathetic society, kickstarting radical thought into a sphere higher than at the end of the 1960s. But the world of punk at first seemed very strange to outsiders. Many people – not just members of straight society but fans of Peter Frampton and Bad Company and Genesis (though perhaps they were one and the same...) and rock critics as well – genuinely were frightened of the punks they passed in the street: no-one had bothered to explain to them that a large part of its origins was art-school dressing-up.

For a time it really did seem like Anarchy In The UK. At the Roxy, the London punk temple, audiences would express their enthusiasm with a constant spray of spit – a bizarre trend soon copied across the country as a hail of gob would be expectorated in the direction of punk acts throughout their stage sets. This paradox of appreciative spit was just one example of the contradictions that formed the glue of punk: on one hand this new tribal grouping was a complete joke in which nothing was taken seriously; whilst at precisely the same moment it was a genuinely radical movement of heartfelt, passionate sincerity. '*We don't care*,' screamed Johnny Rotten, whilst actually caring with the very deepest of feelings. Often branded as a negative, destructive force, punk was in fact the most stridently positive street level artistic statement of the twentieth century, far outweighing the impact of dada or surrealism, its antecedents. As Carl Jung once wrote, all great truths must end in paradox.

ANARCHY IN THE UK

SEX PIST

DAMNED
AND FROM THE USA

JOHNNY & THE
(EX NEW

With Special G

the CL

THE TOUR D

Fri 3 Dec Norwich University
Sat 4 Kings Hall Derby
Sun 5 City Hall Newcastle on Tyne
Leeds Polytechnic
Mon 6 Bowl Bourne mouth
Tue 7
Circus Manchester
Mon 20 Ballroom Torquay
21 Woods Centre Ply

PERMANENT

ents
on U.E.A.

1

LES JEUX
DU
SEXE

Left: *Malcolm McLaren: Cosmic prankster? Or cynical exploitation merchant? Both probably. The name of his management operation, Glitterbest, was, in the circumstances, about as ironic as possible.*

BRATING DOWN
ROXY WITH

ATORS
ON
DAY
EB.

OYAL
D

THURSDAY
3RD
MARCH

WAYN

OH MY DEARS
LOOK
WHAT'S
COMING
SOON

The HEARTBREAKERS

WEDNESDAY
MARCH 2ND

6   VIBRATORS & G.B.H.
7   REGGAE - RECORD NIGHT
8   THE BOYS
9   CORTINAS & BOMBERS

Twenty years on it is hard to imagine the extraordinary and remarkable effect that punk had on British, American, and then world culture. Through an intriguing synchronicity the movement precisely (un)paralleled the cod patriotism fanatically afforded the Silver Jubilee celebrations for Queen Elizabeth II; amongst the many conspiracy theories that bound together punk culture, perhaps the least insane was that the British pop charts had been fixed to prevent 'God Save the Queen' by the Sex Pistols being the number one record during Jubilee week.

The nationalism consciously brewed up by this 'royal event' was sickening, loathsome. Only those who were deeply psychologically blocked by an excess of patriotic street parties, mired in a myopic nostalgia for a Britain that never really was, could have failed to note that the tension imploding in habitually repressed Britain as 7 June 1977 - Jubilee Day - approached was nearly beyond belief. It broke out in the attack by the police on the Sex Pistols' boat party, held on the Thames on the same day.

Among those arrested was Malcolm McLaren, the manager of the Sex Pistols, who claimed to be fascinated with situationism, the confrontational revolutionary French movement that had been at the core of the May 1968 Parisian riots.

With his unruly bush of flaming red hair, pinched lips and exaggeratedly angular facial features, Malcolm McLaren took on the appearance of a character from myth: one part Beelzebub, one part clown-like prankster, this King's Road shopkeeper lived life as the archetypal bad boy at school, a king of aggressive absurdity. This slightly camp figure was a complex character; more intellect than instinct, a Machiavellian character who was the personification of punk paradox.

Self-justifying almost beyond belief, especially when it came to talk of Sid Vicious's pathetic end, he nonetheless set in motion a train of events that altered the course of the last quarter of the twentieth century. In fact, what happened in London in 1977 can seem like an art-school version of May 1968, with events whipped up by an adept *agent provacateur*.

If there was one thing that was especially distasteful about Malcolm McLaren, it was his sense of immoral superiority. McLaren was never one to let an inconvenience like truth interfere with his furthering of the punk plot - something common to several of the key characters, many of whom consistently laid down a complex smokescreen of lies about their pasts. With McLaren it was generally more specific: throughout the course of 1977, for example, McLaren insisted that the Pistols were banned from

playing in London. This was simply not true. In fact, there were no applications to the Greater London Council for a Sex Pistols gig in London in 1977. Had the group played regularly in Britain, might they not have been saved from the sad end to which they were headed throughout that year?

More simply, however, Malcolm McLaren was like a personification of the mood in the collective unconscious of the West – that popular culture was crap, that a change had to come. Whether they realised it or not, everyone was waiting for something like the Sex Pistols. The aroma of decay everywhere was simply too pungent.

The music scene was simply *b-o-r-i-n-g* – the petulant schoolkid word that was central to the punk vocabulary, especially when employed in the phrase *boring old fart*, essentially applicable to anyone not involved in the punk movement. (Quite soon the word *boring* became itself rather boring...)

But there were exceptions. The New York Dolls, who were to become one of the most influential groups of all time, sprang out of a Manhattan-based band called Actress. Actress at first consisted of guitarists Rick Rivets and Arthur Kane and drummer Billy Murcia. When they were joined by bassist Johnny Volume (aka John Genzale jr), he soon decided to become the more tangy Johnny Thunders, switched instruments with Arthur Kane, and began to dominate the group. Not long after Rick Rivets was replaced by Sylvain Sylvain (aka Ronald Mizrahi). In November 1971, they were joined by a singer called David Johansen.

On 13 June 1972, the New York Dolls began a seventeen-week Tuesday residency at Manhattan's Mercer Arts Centre, a dilapidated building of spaces for new groups, art exhibits, avant-garde films and the like. For the first six shows they were billed as the Dolls of New York. But no matter: this group were a revelation amidst the prevalent miasma of weary 'progressive' rock; the frenetic urgency of songs like 'Jet Boy' earned them critical adoration. An immense influence on punk rock, the New York Dolls were, among other things, a glam rock pastiche of the Rolling Stones. Lipstick, high heels, satin and leather were the dress code, as though they had stepped out of the Stones' poster for 'Have You Seen Your Mother'. David Johansen, the singer, was visually and vocally a clone of Mick Jagger; his songwriting partner, Johnny Thunders, similarly established himself as a cartoon version of Keith Richards. Not only were the New York Dolls' songs quintessentially sharp and to the point and – flying in the face of 'progressive' developments – very short, but they also had suitably precise titles: 'Pills', 'Personality Crisis', 'Subway Train', 'Bad Girl', to name just a few.

No-one was ever more determinedly anti-hippie in their dress style than the Dolls. Part of the look was its mixture of cowboy gear with 1940s and 1950s women's clothing. As well as the enormous platform-sole shoes and boots into which all the group stuffed their feet, for example, Arthur Kane would wear a tutu and ballet tights; meanwhile, Johnny Thunders' hair was the ultimate exaggeration of the Rod Stewart teased look – down the back there would be dyed a bright blond streak: and he would put on a girl's blouse with a woman's rhinestone vest over it.

But the greatest influence that the Dolls had on dresswear came from a more oblique angle. A Puerto Rican friend of theirs called Frenchy had a second-hand clothing shop from which he would gladly give them garments. After a time, he became so attached to the group members that he would travel with them to all their shows.

As this antique clothing was somewhat fragile, it was forever splitting and tearing. Accordingly, Frenchy always carried with him a pocketful of safety pins for instant repairs. Turning this adversity into an advantage, the Dolls flaunted such ripped, safety-pinned clothing. It was something that was to impress very much indeed a London clothes-shop owner called Malcom McLaren who briefly became their manager.

Left: *Johnny Thunders.*

Opposite: *Too Much Too Soon? The New York Dolls (left to right) Jerry Nolan, Sylvain Sylvain, David Johansen, Johnny Thunders and Arthur Kane.*

'When I first heard rock and roll,' Malcolm McLaren told *Spin* magazine, 'I think it was *Rock Around The Clock*, and that was back in the mid-fifties in England. The first time I saw a teddy boy, it provoked in me sheer menace, so much that I crossed the road to get out of his way. The badness that it managed to promote made me love the clothes that this chap wore and helped make me understand that you could actually look bad – not be it. I realised fashion could provoke something that made you look completely out of step with everything else that people were terming good. In other words, you became an outsider. That made me fit in. The Sex Pistols was me when it was bad and something else when it was good. The colour black, if it could be defined as a colour, meant to me something very warm and very, very beautiful. The name came about by the idea of a pistol, a pin-up, a young thing, a better-looking assassin, a Sex Pistol. I launched that idea in the form of a band of kids who could be deduced as being bad. When I discovered that the kids had the same anger, could wear black, it was perfect.'

Vivienne Westwood, once a Sunday school teacher.

Though they were by far its sharpest blade, the Dolls were not alone out there on the cutting edge. On 17 October 1972, for example, Roy Hollingworth, *Melody Maker*'s man in New York, had come across a singer called Wayne County. He was wearing 'lipstick and eyeshadow, carrying a handbag and wearing wobbling high-heeled ladies shoes...a feather hat topped a lush brunette wig which fell abundantly over a pinkish baby-doll nightdress, which in turn barely covered a lovely pair of legs encased in ruddy-coloured stockings atop a pair of dainty high heels'. At the end of his show, reported Hollingworth, Wayne County was about to perform a number sitting on a toilet when the power was cut.

That same night a group called Suicide played at the Oscar Wilde room at the Mercer Arts Center. Suicide were two people, one mike, and three keyboards. They described their performance as 'Punk, Funk and Sewer Music by Suicide'. Clearly something was going on in the seamy underbelly of New York's avant garde.

And in October 1972, the leading contenders in this somewhat bizarre Big Apple sideshow were briefly transported to London. On the 29th of that month, the New York Dolls played in London, at a rock'n'roll revival show, billed between the Faces and Ladbroke Grove amphetamine crazies the Pink Fairies.

On that trip the group paid a visit to the King's Road clothing shop run by Malcolm McLaren and Vivienne Westwood. Located at number 430, this establishment was at the unfashionable end of the street that at the end of the 1960s had become the zenith of Swinging London. On a corner known as World's End, like a bald statement of an apocalyptic reality, the shop at the time was trading under the name of 'Let It Rock', a tribute to the Chuck Berry song.

'It took the Dolls to really turn my head around,' McLaren told the *NME*'s Nick Kent in 1976. 'I mean, one day... I'd never heard of 'em before... but they all trouped into the shop in their high-heeled shoes and I was immediately very impressed by the way they handled themselves.

'There were all these Teds 'anging around, thinking what the hell are these geezers doing here? But the Dolls didn't care at all. David Johanssen just went ahead and tried on a drape jacket while Johnny Thunders was over by the juke-box looking for some Eddie Cochran records...I was really taken aback.'

The group stayed on in London. A week later, on 6 November 1972, the group's drummer Billy Murcia went round early one afternoon to the home of an acquaintance. There he engaged in the then chic London practice of swallowing a handful of Mandrax and forcing himself to stay awake. By early evening he had passed out. Attempting to revive him in a cold bath, his hosts forced coffee down his throat: Murcia choked on it and died.

Suicide is painless...and occasionally a bleedin' racket: gobbed on mercilessly in their UK baptism of fire on the Clash's July 1978 Out on Parole tour.

Debbie Harry on life pre-punk: 'I was into junk. I was really fucked up. For a time, it was pretty blank. For a long time I tried to blank out whole blocks of my life. I did junk for about three years, that was right after Wind in the Willows broke up.'

There was always this darker side to the influence of the Rolling Stones on the New York Dolls. And it wasn't restricted to the death of Billy Murcia. In the early 1970s, part of the kudos enjoyed by the Stones was derived from a twisted form of romantic machismo that justified Keith Richards' serious heroin habit as a kind of rebellious glamour. What could be more inevitable than that an impressionable young man like Johnny Thunders, from the rundown Queens district of New York, would aspire to emulate his guitar-playing role model by similarly becoming a junkie?

This was later to have a bad effect on the London punk scene. Although the Rolling Stones would be publicly denounced, many punks were secretly very impressed indeed with the death-wish habit of one of the group's members.

By 19 December 1972, the Dolls had a new drummer, Jerry Nolan, with whom they played for the first time that night at Mercer Arts Center.

By the time the New York Dolls eponymously titled album was released in the United States, on 27 July 1973, they were the fulcrum of an entire scene: support acts for the Dolls over the last few months had included Suicide, Jonathan Richman and the Modern Lovers, and Wayne County. Both the Mercer Arts Center and Max's Kansas City had become happening spots - the Dolls would also often play at the Diplomat Hotel. Other acts in this loosely-structured, quasi-boho world included the Harlots of 42nd Street, Teenage Lust, and the Planets.

And there were other tremors: a couple of months previously Richard Meyers and Tom Miller, who would soon change their names to Richard Hell and Tom Verlaine, were looking for a guitarist for their group, the Neon Boys. One person they turned down was called Doug Colvin, who was later to achieve fame as Dee Dee Ramone. 'We had two songs with just three straightforward chords apiece and he couldn't figure out what the hell they were,' Verlaine later complained, perhaps missing the point. The sole recorded output from the Neon Boys was a rough demo of a Richard Hell song, charmingly entitled 'Love Comes In Spurts'.

Meanwhile, making their debut at the Bobern Tavern in October, 1973, were the Stilettos, fronted by Debbie Harry, with occasional guitarist Chris Stein. Harry had previously played in a group called Wind in the Willows.

Wayne County, who later became Jayne - big in Germany...

19

Talking Heads (left to right: Jerry Harrison, David Byrne, Chris Frantz, Tina Weymouth), probably the most artistically satisfying of all punk acts: did the sense of nagging austerity in their sound have anything to do with Byrne having been born in Scotland?

Tina Weymouth: 'There was a time when we felt like people pretending to be a band. Then all of a sudden we realised we were a band.'

David Byrne: 'I really like New York. It's the kind of place where you see anything happen, y'know. Just looking out the window, you see people, uh, falling over! Yeah, people fall over all the time in New York. No one gives a damn. It's great.'

Tina Weymouth: 'The aesthetic was called Mondo and there was a lot of black leather. The Artistics wore all black and David also had a leopard–skin guitar. They did a lot of cover songs – some Troggs songs, "96 Tears", The Knickerbockers' "Lies" – and one original. "Sick Boy", "Spin Spin", and also "I'm Not In Love" existed at that time but in a more primitive form. It was very very loud. You couldn't stand closer than fifty feet to the band because it was so loud it was abusive. At one party in a concrete loft everybody was just squished into one corner because of the noise.'

In January 1975 Talking Heads started rehearsing on the Lower East Side into which they had moved. By now Tina Weymouth was playing bass. They rehearsed until May. Two blocks up from where they were living was a joint called CBGBs. Tina Weymouth: 'Although Patti Smith had played there and attracted a SoHo and St Mark's art clique, it didn't really have its own crowd – just band's friends and musicians, who came mainly because it was the only place to play original music.'

Getting an act of sorts together at the Rhode Island School of Design in Providence were the Artistics, featuring David Byrne and Chris Frantz. Amongst their friends was a bass-player, Martina (Tina) Weymouth, who helped Chris and David write their first original song, 'Psycho Killer'. Moving to New York in September of 1974 they became Talking Heads.

David Byrne: '"Psycho Killer" is the first song I ever wrote. It was sometime in 1973, I guess, because Chris Frantz and I had got this band called the Artistics together. Later we changed to the Autistics because somebody, I think, misunderstood us when we told them our name...there were two guitars, bass and drums and the guitarists were me and this other guy who was autistic, so that sort of stuck. Unfortunately.

'We didn't look much different than we do now....there were some Smokey Robinson songs we did. Things like "Tears Of A Clown" and "My Baby Must Be A Magician". I think we did "The Love I Saw In You Was Just A Mirage" as well...Then there was "1-2-3 Red Light", and this old 1910 Fruitgum Company song which we carried through to playing at early Talking Heads' dates. "96 Tears"? Yeah, we played that too, I think. "Psychotic Reaction" we definitely played.'

Byrne had been studying a conceptual arts course, but was turned off the elitism implicit within it. One way of displaying his contempt for this was to shave off his hair and beard onstage to the accompaniment of an accordianist and a girl displaying cue cards in Russian. (Some may have felt this way of making a complaint was much the same as what he was protesting about...)

21

On a purely publicity level, it was certainly to the advantage of the whole scene that Patti Smith and Tom Verlaine were for a time a woosome twosome, with photographs of the pert pair pictured together in such publications as *Rock Scene.*

Patti Smith, punk's poet laureate.

In January 1974 the Ramones had formed in New York. Johnny (John Cummings) and Dee Dee (Douglas Colvin) got together with Joey (Jeff Hyman) who played drums. At the end of March, the Ramones made their stage debut, at the Performance Studio on East 23rd Street. In July, however, they made a radical and crucial change in direction. The group's manager, Tommy Erdleyi, persuaded Joey he should be the singer instead of the drummer. Then Tommy took up the drumsticks himself, becoming Tommy Ramone.

Part of the Ramones' publicity schtick was that the group were genuinely stupid and cretinous, that they were only able to use words of one syllable or less. Somehow this was construed as a compliment, as though it bestowed upon them an even greater credibility. Needless to say, this made one suspect that they secretly all had PhDs.

The previous month the Patti Smith Group - Patti Smith, Lenny Kaye, Richard Sohl on keyboards - had gone into Electric Ladyland, appropriately enough as it had been set up by Jimi Hendrix, and recorded 'Hey Joe', a tribute to formerly kidnapped and now guerrilla heiress Patty Hearst. Since her first poetry reading in Manhattan's St Mark's Place on 10 February 1971, Smith had been the darling of the New York underground, energetically pushed by the influential journalist Lisa Robinson, who managed to straddle this boho scene and that of instant pop culture. One of Smith's poems was entitled 'Oath' and began with the line, 'Jesus died for somebody's sins, but not mine'. This was the line she would eventually use as the introduction to her version of 'Gloria'.

On 2 March 1975, Television played their first ever gig at the eighty-eight-seat Townhouse Theatre on 46th Street in Manhattan. The Neon Boys had moved on - though at this stage Tom Verlaine and Richard Hell remained musical compadres.

On 20 June the Ramones and Talking Heads shared the bill at CBGBs. The following week both groups appeared there again, at what was billed as the Summer Rock Festival. As a consequence of a review from a *Village Voice* reporter, entitled 'The conservative impulse of the new Rock underground', Talking Heads appeared on the cover of the *Voice*. In October the Ramones signed to the then little-known Sire Records, run by Seymour and Linda Stein. Their first album was recorded in eighteen hours.

A distinctly alternative rock'n'roll word was not restricted to New York. In Paris there was already a scene actually calling itself 'punk'. Central to it was Marc Zermati, who ran Skydog Records from his shop in the Les Halles district, at the time the focal point of the French rock'n'roll scene. To some extent it was also the headquarters for French punk.

Punk first emerged in Paris around 1973, influenced by the adoration of style-obsessed Parisians for the likes of Lou Reed - the principal visual role model - and the Doors and Flamin Groovies, and by the seminal punk rock'n'roll writings of Yves Adrian in France's monthly *Rock Et Folk*. By that year Parisian groovers were already wearing the kind of black biker-leather jackets and tight pants that would emerge as part of the uniform of Malcolm McLaren's shocktroops. 'In Paris in 1973,' Marc Zermati remembered, 'we were calling ourselves Punks. We were very fond of those pre-psychedelic American bands like Shadows of Knight. In fact, the first time I met Malcolm McLaren was when he came into my shop in Paris when he had come over to see the New York Dolls. The scene in Paris was really moving at the time. There was a lot of action. It's funny that in the end it happened instead on a really large scale in London.'

Considered really to be a sort of more druggy (heroin was considered very chic in Paris) sub-division of Glam-rock, this scene's influence had all the same filtered back to London. The result was that by 1975, a small London circle brought together such diverse elements as Roxy Music and their entourage, pub rockers with an art-school edge like Kilburn and the Highroads and - to a lesser extent - the Winkies, as well as the Malcolm McLaren fashion circus. Chris Thomas, later to become producer of both the Sex Pistols and the Pretenders,

remembered that the previous year this scene had been characterised 'by several girls who only wore black leather and spoke with foreign accents' . Straight-legged jeans from Fiorucci were also very popular.

The visit to Paris by Malcolm McLaren to which Marc Zermati referred had occurred on the second trip to Europe by the New York Dolls. On 10 May 1974, they had released their second album, 'Too Much Too Soon' - in the review of the record in *Rolling Stone*, they had been called 'the best hard rock band in America'.

By now McLaren had become a born again rock'n'roller: the New York Dolls had rekindled within him the same blood-tingling excitement he had felt from the likes of Eddie Cochran and the great British rocker Billy Fury (about whom he had tried to make a film whilst at Croydon art school), which he had lost when the late 1960s ushered in the era of album-dominated Rock. He followed them around London and Paris, almost awestruck.

The ultimate consequence of this epiphany-like experience was that in early 1975 McLaren journeyed to New York to take over the management of the New York Dolls for some months, attempting to slow the final disintegration of this seminal group via the injection of a new radical image. The manifesto was stated in a press release: 'What are the politics of boredom? Better Red Than Dead. Contrary to the vicious lies, the New York Dolls have not disbanded, and having completed the first Red, 3-D Rock'n'roll movie entitled *Trash*, have in fact, assumed the role of the "People's Information Collective" in direct association with the Red Guard.'

This re-make re-model of the Dolls' persona was unveiled for a show in New York at the Hippodrome on 28 February; citizens of the United States had been thoroughly programmed with regard to how they should think about the Red 'menace' - which meant that their hammer and sickle backdrop was just about the last straw for the Dolls in their own country. 'With the Dolls,' McLaren told me, 'I did the whole thing - red vinyl, Chairman Mao, end of the Vietnam war. I've always related music to clothes.' Not for the first time, Malcolm McLaren went too far.

Opening for the Dolls at the Hippodrome that night was Television, the moody, nagging group started by Tom Verlaine and Richard Hell; at the time they were considered the most happening new group in New York. McLaren was greatly taken with Hell in particular, especially his look: a torn T-shirt, safety pins, and cut-up hair. In fact, McLaren went so far as to suggest that he take Hell to England to become his manager. Hell, however, declined the offer. Dispirited because his new songs were hardly being played in Television, he had decided to quit the group. In fact, Richard Hell had ironically already been talking about getting a group together with Johnny Thunders and Jerry Nolan.

Travelling with McLaren to play in Florida, the Dolls finally broke up in Miami on 24 April 1975: Johnny Thunders and Jerry Nolan announced that they were leaving the group. Six days later, on 30 April 1975, the Heartbreakers, featuring Thunders, Nolan and Richard Hell, made their debut at Club 82 in New York.

Jerry Nolan: 'David (Johansen) was still stuck on "Personality Crisis" and me and Johnny wanted to get a whole new thing together, so we rang up Richard Hell who had just split from his band, got Walter Lure on guitar and that was the original Heartbreakers.'

'CATCH THEM WHILE THEY'RE STILL ALIVE' -
early 1976 poster for Richard Hell-era Heartbreakers

In 1975 Island Records A&R man Richard Williams sent Brian Eno over to New York to produce some demos of Television. They didn't work out, however. 'Eno is just an experimenter,' complained Tom Verlaine. '...He's an intellectual, and I really don't think we are. He thought we were, and we're not. I just want a commercial sound.'

Opposite: *Television's 'Marquee Moon' was a masterly work, though they proved unable to repeat it.*

Tom Verlaine: 'I guess if we have one big thing we would like to get across, it's that we all have the goodness about New York, you know the thing that the Velvets had, or John Coltrane...that whole element. But we aren't limited by it, and I don't think this is only exclusive to New York.'

Johnny Thunders.

As the Dolls flew into Paris's Orly airport, they were met by a horde of press. Johnny Thunders, feeling distinctly queasy, threw up on the concourse floor just as he arrived in front of these representatives of the Fourth Estate. Malcolm McLaren found this colossally impressive. Here lay the origins of the news reports of the Pistols puking at Heathrow airport at the beginning of 1977 on their way out of Britain to appear in Holland: there was no truth whatsoever in these stories, however.

25

cuttlee

2

John 'Sparko' Sparks, Lee Brilleaux, The Big Figure.

Alternative music in Britain in the early 1970s was restricted to pub rock.
Pub rock was very male, the sound of wet woollen overcoats in November, chaps with right hands wrapped around foaming tankards of light and bitter; a kind of anti-glam-rock. It also removed music from people who would rather roll a joint than down a pint. This had an effect on the music: pub rock was drunken, littered with Chuck Berry riffs, and a little too conscious of its grassroots purpose of reclaiming music for the people.

There were exceptions: for example, the lively triumvirate of Brinsley Schwartz, featuring Nick Lowe, Ducks Deluxe, and Chilli Willi and the Red Hot Peppers, this last act overseen by an energetic young manager called Jake Riviera.

Riviera was also friends with the team that made up the most awesome act in all of pub rock, the only one to break large commercially – the mighty and menacing Dr Feelgood. Hailing from Canvey Island, a flat landscape in the Thames estuary dominated by oil refineries, this four-piece group looked a revelation: narrow lapelled, tight-trousered suits, short hair, jailbird psychosis in the eyes. Quite a feat of method acting, considering that Wilko Johnson, the extraordinarily gifted guitarist, was a lover of William Blake and had travelled the hippie trail to India. Singer Lee Brilleaux equally had the betting-shop appearance of a salesman of used cars of dubious origin, his skinny ties a trademark. Drummer The Big Figure and bass-player John 'Sparko' Sparks simply looked like thugs (though weren't, of course).

With their three-minute choppy r'n'b songs and charity shop image, the Feelgoods were a colossal influence on British Punk groups. Despite – or because of – their appearance of overt surliness, they had an aura of approachability, a sense of being one of us, at the same time as being totally unique.

Wherever they played – the Kensington, the Hope and Anchor in Islington, even the occasional 'prestige' gig at Dingwall's Dancehall – songs like 'Roxette', 'She Does It Right', and 'Back in the Night' pulled in an audience ready to be mesmerised by Wilko's whiplash stage moves, like a performance-art variation on Chuck Berry's celebrated duckwalk. Wilko's tendency towards a petulant jawline, which was often really introversion sparked off by an excessive ingestion of hashish (Lebanese gold was at the time very popular, courtesy, it was always said, of the PLO), contributed towards elements of onstage moodiness that delighted audiences and came to be considered as part of the show. 'Wobbler, wobbler,' audiences would happily gasp at the least sign of Wilko walking offstage.

Paul Weller: 'I used to love Wilko, he was like the English Chuck Berry. I went to see them in the Guildford Civic. He came out, did this huge lick with his legs out and they were off. Yeah! It's like that Lennon quote when he went to see a rock'n'roll movie and he thought, Now that's a good job, I'd like to do that.'

Wilko Johnson, a fine testament to a love of William Blake.

Unsurprisingly, the Feelgoods' most successful record was a live album, 'Stupidity', which entered the UK chart at number one when it was released in the autumn of 1976: in the *NME* feature to promote its release, Lee Brilleaux shared a split front cover with a certain Johnny Rotten.

The resulting financial windfall from their success was not frittered away, but used in the most advisable manner: for example, when his old mate Jake Riviera came round trying to borrow four hundred notes to start a record company he wanted to call Stiff Records, Lee Brilleaux coughed up on the spot.

Amongst established acts the only sign of creative life seemed to be in the Sensational Alex Harvey Band, which had come together extremely successfully in 1972, a fusion of a young Glasgow group called Tear Gas with veteran r'n'b singer Alex Harvey. The group's dramatic concept was ambitious, a mix of rock, r'n'b, and British music hall; early audiences were polarised, traditionalists managing to feel affronted. Several successful albums followed, and a number of chart singles, including an absurd version of the Tom Jones hit 'Delilah'. With the foil of guitarist Zal Cleminson, a fantasy figure in clown make-up, Harvey's live performances certainly lived up to the superlative in the name of the group - generally, they really were sensational, and quite revolutionary. An aspiring rock'n'roll guitarist called Mick Jones, and his friends Tony James and Paul Simonon would frequently be in SAHB London audiences. Jones and James were also deeply influenced by Mott The Hoople, Ian Hunter's rumbustious bunch of rock'n'rollers.

At a lesser level, one Declan (McManus) Costello was playing around south-west London as a solo act. On 4 July 1973, Steve Jones and Paul Cook stole the microphones from David Bowie's final shows of his 1973 tour, preparing for an as-yet-unnamed project. In other Glam-rock news, Brian Eno had been fired from Roxy Music that same month: the fact that the first man positively to celebrate his non-musician status was pushed from the group by his rival Bryan Ferry only increased Eno's heroic stature in the eyes of the masses.

Also in July, 1973, Kilburn and the High Roads, the only group with enough character to rival Dr Feelgood, signed to Raft Records; the group's singer Ian Dury was like an homage to Gene Vincent, another product of Britain's art-college system, a man with an immense knowledge of r'n'b and jazz. The Kilburns had played their first show as long ago as 5 December 1971, at Croydon School of Art. As well as Dury, the band was made up of Russell Hardy on piano, Ian Smith on bass, Terry Day on drums, Davey Payne on sax and Ted Speight on guitar.

By the beginning of 1974, pub rock was starting to admit some new contenders. On 17 January 1974, for example, Johnny Sox played at the Newlands Tavern, Peckham. This group had recently moved from Sweden to London, fronted by Englishman Hugh Cornwell. After a handful of dates, Johnny Sox split up and Cornwell started up a group that he called the Guildford Stranglers.

By August that year a group called The 101 All Stars, featuring a singer called John 'Woody' Mellors, was beginning to play in some of London's rougher pubs.

Things hotted up in Britain during 1975, small seeds scattered all about. At the end of February, for example, Brinsley Schwartz announced that the group was suspending operations as a touring outfit, although their bass-player Nick Lowe hoped to continue songwriting. In May the Stranglers (formerly the Guildford Stranglers) added keyboards-player Dave Greenfield, giving their sound its Gothic, Doors-like wash.

Wilko meets Ian Dury live.

Rotten: I saw Iggy Pop at Kings Cross - so there! Before he was trendy...and he was awful. Embarrassing. Then that sort of thing became acceptable... Outrageous. God, all the people who were on and no-one even bothered to look at them twice. And now you can't get near them.
'Lou Reed. Yeah, I remember that. Complete lack of interest from the audience... Most people had vague ideas of what the Velvet Underground were, but had never heard them.'

Rotten: 'Roxy, I liked Roxy Music. They were good. Loony. Ferry singing his songs in a dinner jacket was completely berserk. And then he took his image seriously. Funny that. They all crack up over that. End up believing in their publicity themselves.'

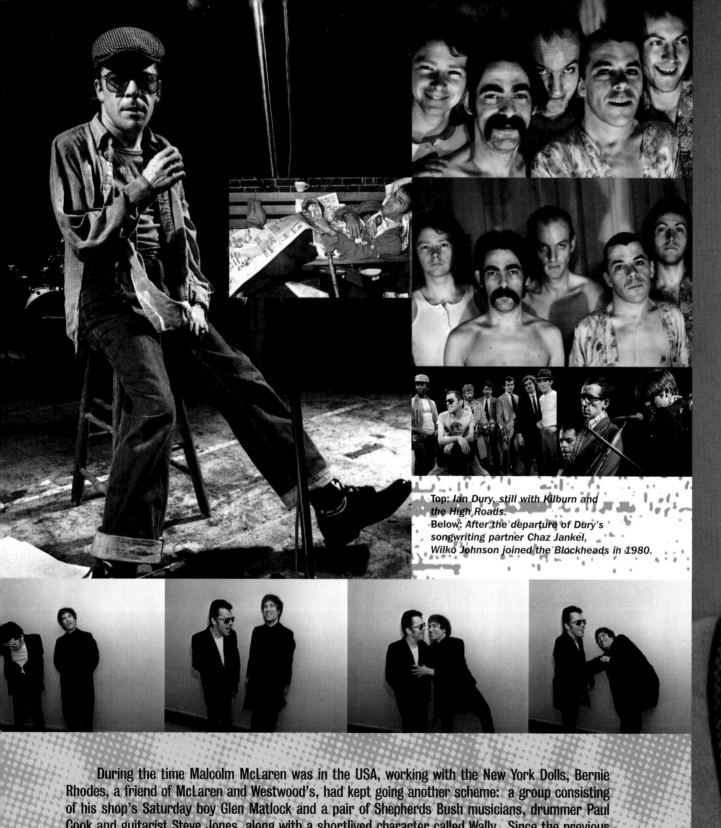

Top: *Ian Dury, still with Kilburn and the High Roads.*
Below: *After the departure of Dury's songwriting partner Chaz Jankel, Wilko Johnson joined the Blockheads in 1980.*

During the time Malcolm McLaren was in the USA, working with the New York Dolls, Bernie Rhodes, a friend of McLaren and Westwood's, had kept going another scheme: a group consisting of his shop's Saturday boy Glen Matlock and a pair of Shepherds Bush musicians, drummer Paul Cook and guitarist Steve Jones, along with a shortlived character called Wally. Since the previous year they had been nagging McLaren for help in forming a group: all that McLaren had provided so far had been a name, the Sex Pistols – Let It Rock had subsequently been re-named Sex.

But in August 1975 Bernie found a scrawny kid called John Lydon who walked into Sex wearing

In a throwaway review in the NME by a young American called Chriss Hynde of a record by the De Franco Family, she framed the following prescient sentence: 'The only way for a new rock consciousness to surface from the dark ruins of the Beatle phenomenon is for some ballsy teen to step up front and declare war with a defiant "Move over!"'

Left: Ian Dury, the 'Godfather of Punk' poses in front of the poster for his seminal 'New Boots & Panties' LP.

31

That summer John 'Woody' Mellors had moved back to London from Newport in Wales: he had gone there because he didn't have anywhere else to live and had been the singer with an r'n'b group called the Vultures. In London in 1972, he'd busked - on a ukelele! - in the London Underground, assisted by an old tube platform performer called Tymon Dogg. Back in the capital he moved into a squat at 101 Walterton Road in Maida Vale, and with the other people living there formed the 101 All Stars, who soon became known simply as the 101'ers. By February of the next year, he had re-styled himself as Joe Strummer, refusing to respond to anyone who addressed him as Woody.

Rotten: 'You have to appreciate about Bernie, that he does talk. And so do I: I talk myself into death traps sometimes. And that's what Bernie does. And it hurts him. I know how much he influenced Malcolm. He made all Malcolm's shirts. He did all the t-shirt designs. It's not that Bernie was Malcolm's stooge at all. It was the other way around.'

a Pink Floyd T-shirt with the words 'I hate...' added above the group's name. Rhodes invited Lydon to come and meet Malcolm in the Roebuck pub. Lydon auditioned for the Pistols by miming to the pub's jukebox. 'Bernie definitely influenced the start of the Pistols,' Lydon told me in 1980 for The Face. 'He got me in the band. Malcolm hated my guts, because of the way me and Sid used to take the piss out of him.'

The same month that Rhodes found John Lydon, McLaren and Vivienne Westwood were charged with a breach of public decency: the T-shirts they were selling of pantless cowboys, their penises almost touching, were too much for the forces of law and order.

On 6 November 1975, the Sex Pistols played their first ever show at St Martin's Art College in London's West End: five songs into the set the plug was pulled; among the numbers were covers of the Who's 'Substitute' and the Small Faces' 'Whatcha Gonna Do About It', in which Johnny Rotten, as he had become known, swopped the word 'hate' for 'love' in the line 'I want you to know that I love you'. The next day the group played another show, at Central School of Art And Design. They got through a thirty-minute set.

Bernard Rhodes, popularly known as "Bernie" (to his chagrin: 'I'm not a taxi driver'), was an ex-Mod who had been involved on the fringes of the music business, working in various ill-defined roles, with the Who amongst other acts. More recently running rock'n'roll clothes shop Granny Takes A Trip, he had of late moved along the street a few doors to Sex. Rhodes had long been friends with Malcolm McLaren: a popular story, a justification for their claims to be situationists, was that they had met during the May 1968 riots in Paris - although neither of them was in fact there. Working with McLaren and Westwood, Bernie had come up with some of the most striking T-shirt designs, notably the one in late 1974 that cried out: 'You're gonna wake up one morning and *know* what side of the bed you've been lying on'.

At Sex Rhodes saw himself as a kind of creative advisor. There were those, however, who felt that McLaren and Westwood saw him only as a shop assistant, a point emphasised when Malcolm McLaren resolutely turned down Rhodes' request for a partnership. For his part, Rhodes felt fully justified in such a request: not only had he helped run the shop whilst McLaren was in the States with the Dolls, but he had also discovered John Lydon and kept the Pistols going during this time.

Such an alliance might have been a perfect marriage. McLaren was weasely, cold and stingy; Rhodes was runty, warm and stingy. Each had similar skills: an engagingly slick verbal hustle, a serious sense of the askew, and a surreal humour. When McLaren's back was to the wall, however, this last would desert him utterly, leading to crass decisions like the Ronnie Biggs-meets-the-Sex-Pistols episode.

Mick Jones, Paul Simonon and Joe Strummer hold a camera-shy Bernie Rhodes back so that this picture can be taken for posterity.

apocalypse NOW

3

London SS is one of the great mythological groups of all time, a legend only enhanced by the fact that it never played a single show. It was formed by Mick Jones, a guitar-playing art student who had been born in Brixton; after living with his grandmother in a towerblock off the Harrow Road, he had moved in 1975 to a small flat in Highgate.

Jones had first been in a group called the Delinquents, then becoming part of Little Queenie, initially managed by Tony Gordon, who went on to manage Sham 69 and Culture Club. Soon, however, Mick Jones fell out with the group. Kelvin Blacklock, the Little Queenie singer, introduced Jones to Tony James, a bass-playing maths student at Brunel university, who was trying, via the Musicians Wanted section in *Melody Maker*, to form a group.

At the Nashville one night Mick Jones and Tony James went to watch The 101'ers. They hated the group, who seemed to this style-obsessed pair to be an archetypal pub-rock outfit. But they were impressed with the singer. At the gig that evening they ran into a short, bespectacled man with an extremely protruberant nose - Bernie Rhodes.

Jones was wearing one of the pink T-shirts from Sex that bore the legend 'You're gonna wake up one morning and *know* what side of the bed you've been lying on'. And so was Rhodes. 'We said, "Go on, stand over there in that T-shirt," remembered James. 'Fuck off!' replied Rhodes. 'I made it.' Impressed, the pair found themselves in conversation with this gnome-like fellow, who gave them their first information about a new group that was forming called the Sex Pistols; he told them of Malcolm McLaren's role in setting it up.

In 1981 Jones told the *NME*'s Paul Rambali about his first impressions of Bernie Rhodes: 'I thought he was a piano player. He seemed like a really bright geezer. We got on like a house on fire.'

Like everyone did, Mick Jones and Tony James first of all genuflected to McLaren - he made an impact on impressionable young men because of the role he had had with the New York Dolls. ('That was Bernie's paranoia: that he was always in Malcolm's shadow.' - Tony James.) For the Pistols, McLaren had bought a rehearsal studio in Denmark Street, London's Tin Pan Alley, for £1,000. 'We went to see Malcolm at the studio,' said James. 'The Pistols were there. We both had really long hair.' McLaren took them for a meal. They were both extremely taken with his vision. Tony James: 'He told us what would happen: that a group would come along and completely shake up the music business and alter things utterly. And it all came true in the most grizzly sense.'

Unfortunately, however, McLaren didn't recognise the potential talents before him. So the pair arranged a more thorough meeting with Bernie Rhodes, telling him of their plans to form a group called London SS.

The 'London' part of the name, of course, alluded to the 'New York' in New York Dolls, whilst the 'SS' initials were a conscious shock tactic, in the same way that Siouxsie's and Sid's later adoption of the swastika had more to do with the defacing of school exercise books than with approbation for fascism. Even if such dark flirting was only symptomatic of puerile rebellion, it all the same remained a loaded gun.

The mood in the slipstream of Glam-rock was one of decadence and amorality. Cavani's *The Night Porter*, starring Dirk Bogarde and Charlotte Rampling, set the tone with its emphasis on the sexual codes contained within Nazi uniforms; cocaine was proclaimed to be the champagne of drugs: but in chic circles there was also dabbling in heroin, personified by Keith Richards' public flaunting of his habit; and the downer Mandrax could be an after-dinner treat at chic west London parties.

'Bernie made us go up to the Bull and Bush in Shepherd's Bush, which was unbelievably rough and dangerous. As soon as he got there he slapped all this Nazi regalia on the table: "If you're going to call yourself London SS, you'll have to deal with this." We hadn't thought at all about the Nazi implications. It just seemed like a very anarchic, stylish thing to do,' admitted James.

After McLaren had turned down his request for a half-share in the Pistols, Bernie Rhodes had set about looking for a group of his own. Following their meeting with him, Mick Jones and Tony James quickly placed an advertisement in the Musicians Wanted section in *Melody Maker* - 'Decadent 3rd generation rock and roll image essential. New York Dolls style.' Jones was still living in Highgate and it was the phone number of this address that was given in the ad. James lived in Twickenham, at the physically most distant end from Highgate of the 27 bus route: every day he would take the two-hour ride to Jones's home, where they would both sit anxiously by the phone.

Only about half a dozen people - one of whom called from Manchester and was called Steven Morrisey ('I don't think he came down for an audition.' - James) - replied to this ad, however. All the same, Jones and James were extremely taken with the very first response: Brian James was a very rock'n'roll guitarist with a Belgian group called Bastard. As the duo deemed necessary, he was stick-insect thin. (This was always a priority; in *Melody Maker* in November 1975, for example, they ran a further ad: Thin young drummer required - into loud punk rock, MC5/Dolls.) After meeting the pair, Brian James went back to Brussels to quit his group.

Bernie Rhodes found the London SS a rehearsal room, which stank of damp, under a cafe in Praed Street, Paddington.

'When we started working with Bernie, he changed our lives,' said James. 'Up to then we were the New York Dolls, and had never thought of writing more than "Personality Crisis". I remember sitting in the cafe upstairs with Bernie and saying I had an idea for a song about selling rockets in Selfridges. He liked it. But he was thinking of nuclear rockets and I was only thinking of fireworks.

'He said, "You're not going to be able to do anything unless you give me a statement of intent." It was artspeak. He'd give us reading lists: Proust, books on modern art - it was a great education. He also used to pull a sort of class thing: are you street, or are you middle class? It didn't seem very honest, as he was patently obviously middle class himself.'

Through the door of the rehearsal studio wafted various future members of the cast of punk. One Paul Simonon turned up, wanting to be the singer: as a perfect David Bowie lookalike he sang the lyrics '*I'm a roadrunner, I'm a roadrunner*', from the Jonathan Richman song, over and over for ten minutes until he was requested to stop. Both Terry Chimes and Nick Headon auditioned as drummers. Headon was offered the job but left after a week. Having given up the hunt for a singer, London SS started rehearsing with Mick Jones on vocals and a drummer called Roland Hot. Material included MC5's 'Ramblin' Rose', the Strangeloves' 'Night Time' and 'Protex Blue', a Mick Jones original.

When Chris Miller turned up to audition as drummer, at the instigation of Malcolm McLaren, he empathised well with Brian James;

One evening in late summer, 1975, Chris Miller, a former theatre stage manager from Croydon, made his way up to Dingwalls in North London. The Pink Fairies were playing, and Chris felt it his duty to check out the more spirited outfits in what for him had become a terminally boring music scene.

Now at Dingwalls he found himself standing up at the bar next to Malcolm McLaren, Bernie Rhodes' fellow plotter in a loose conspiracy to disrupt the smug, unjustified complacency of the music business. Back in London after his abortive stint with the New York Dolls, McLaren had set about forming the Sex Pistols, who at this stage were still rehearsing. Knowing about the Pistols' scene - 'Which was then very underground - there were only about fifteen people who were actually aware that any of this was going on' - and sensing a kindred spirit, Rat Scabies busied himself with pouring out a diatribe to McLaren about how drab was the then current music. Impressed with Rat's attitude, McLaren asked him for his address and phone number.

He didn't have to wait long for a call. Malcolm McLaren had immediately informed both Chrissie and *NME* writer Nick Kent of his discovery of Rat Scabies. 'He told me,' remembered Chrissie, 'he'd found this incredible drummer for me to play with. Malcolm had decided that he looked like a good drummer - he'd never heard him play.'

Indeed, the very next day after McLaren had met Rat Scabies, the latter was sitting in his 'poxy bedsit' off Portobello Road when there was a ring on the doorbell: 'Malcolm turned up with Chrissie and Nick Kent and asked me if I wanted to drum with them in a group. I'd heard of Nick Kent much more than I

had of Chrissie - in fact, I was quite impressed that he had actually walked into my little bedsit. Chrissie was no one then. I didn't know she'd written for NME. I just thought she was a loud-mouthed American boiler. Really, she looked the same as she does now.'

At the time, her Vivienne Westwood clothes customised by the addition of a black leather jacket - as worn by all Lou Reed-obsessed Parisian exponents of outlaw chic - the appearance of Chrissie Hynde, says Rat, was 'so outrageous. She was the first punk bird - she and Vivienne were, actually, but Vivienne designed the clothes.'

But after a couple of days, Chrissie returned to Rat's flat and told him she had decided she could not work with Kent, a former lover. 'But she said, "Why don't we just go out and hang around somewhere?" So me and Chrissie just used to go and knock about in Soho and the West End and wander around and have a laugh.

'We were completely broke - Chrissie was totally skint: she used to go and model at St Martin's Art College for 75 pence an hour. We just used to wander around going into shops and public places of interest. She spent so much of her time just trying to stay alive. She was sleeping on any floor she could find, though she was staying at Malcolm's a bit, because she and Vivienne were good mates.'

Above: The Damned, the first UK Punk group with record success, but their career soon faltered. From left to right: Captain Sensible, Rat Scabies, Brian James, Dave Vanian. Endlessly breaking up and re-forming, they had a larger run of success in the mid-1980s, even getting a number 3 UK hit with a re-make of Barry Ryan's 'Eloise'. Captain Sensible was briefly a punk superstar after 'Happy Talk', a song from South Pacific, topped the charts in the summer of 1982. In 1996 they were still touring.

his fearsome scratching caused him to get a new name – Rat Scabies. James: 'He genuinely did have scabies. Bernie was paranoid about catching it, and put newspaper on all the chairs.'

A little later Tony James saw the drummer in the Portobello Road pub they used to frequent, on the corner with Westbourne Grove. 'He was wearing a T-shirt that said "Rat Scabies". I thought that was all wrong: it wasn't about being a cartoon figure. On the other hand, I do remember being in that pub one Saturday afternoon when he had a piss in the middle of the bar: He was prepared to do anything – I was very impressed.'

Before Scabies and James could properly link up, however, there was a separate effort at a group, inspired by Malcolm McLaren, who was also using the rehearsal room Rhodes had discovered. He tried out Scabies together with the former Sex shop assistant, Chrissie Hynde, in a group whose line-up and name McLaren had suggested – Masters of the Backside. Chrissie only played guitar, not performing any vocals. The group had not one but two singers: Dave Vanian, a former gravedigger from Hemel Hempstead, who resembled a Regency funeral director; and his vocal sparring partner Dave White, a blond, funny, effeminate character who worked in a King's Road boutique and was the complete visual opposite of Vanian. The bass-player was a suggestion of Rat's, an acquaintance from his home area of Croydon, called Ray Burns, shortly to become known as Captain Sensible.

McLaren had deemed that, pantomime-like, Chrissie Hynde should be dressed as an effeminate male guitarist, and carry a cane with her when she went onstage. 'Malcolm,' explained Rat, 'had the idea that Chrissie should be disguised as a boy, as a very effeminate guitarist.' If the group had managed to make it as far as the stage, part of Chrissie's act was that she would flog the other musicians as they played.

Though studded with future Punk luminaries, Masters of the Backside only worked together for a matter of days. Their material included the Spencer Davis Group's 'Gimme Some Lovin'', the Troggs' classic 'I Can't Control Myself', and even early Pink Floyd material; they also tried out what Rat defined as 'some Chrissie Hynde biker-type songs'.

After a few days' rehearsal, Malcolm McLaren, Vivienne Westwood, and their friend Helen of Troy came to watch them play. 'They laughed their heads off,' Sensible recalled. 'They said it was the funniest thing they had ever seen in their lives. I imagine it would have taken the world by storm if we'd ever got around to playing gigs.'

Instead, however, over Christmas 1975, Rat Scabies went back to playing with guitarist Brian James, taking with him Vanian and Captain Sensible, thereby forming the Damned. 'I went off with Brian James because Chrissie seemed completely talentless on guitar,' admitted Rat.

With regards to the London SS, therefore, it was back to square one for Mick Jones and Tony James - although the Sex Pistols had unsuccessfully attempted to contact Jones, to offer him the role of second guitarist.

Already there was a sense of urgency for Jones and James. Had they missed the boat?

The Sex Pistols, after all, had already played their first shows. And on 21 February 1976 the group received the first music press review of one of their live gigs, a show at the Marquee nine days previously.

For this first ever newspaper write-up, in the *New Musical Express*, the Sex Pistols received an unusually large amount of copy, with a picture of Johnny Rotten at the bottom of the page. The *NME*'s apocalyptic headline was also rather more than such a new group might have expected (McLaren's visits to the *NME* with Nick Kent seemed to have paid off...): 'Don't look over your shoulders, but the Sex Pistols are coming'. Neil Spencer, who wrote the review, defined the group thus: "a quarter [sic] of spiky teenage misfits from the wrong end of various London roads, playing 60s-styled white punk rock as unself-consciously as it's possible to play it these days i.e. self-consciously'.

During 'the moronic "I'm Pretty Vacant", a meandering power-chord job', chairs had started flying around the stage, chucked by Johnny Rotten, the group's singer, Spencer informed the readers. The review was all the more unusual as the Pistols were only the support act, starting the evening for Eddie and the Hotrods, an up and coming Essex group soon to be sold as 'Punk': by the time the Pistols had come offstage, much of the

Hotrods' equipment had been trashed. 'Actually, we're not into music,' one of the group told Spencer, 'we're into chaos.'

On 23 April 1976, it must have been the turn of the Sex Pistols to feel nervous. That day saw the release of 'The Ramones', the first album by the group that was creating a mythology for itself in New York as a kind of Lower East Side set of cartoon-like dunderheads. Although it contained fourteen songs, the LP's total running time was less than twenty-eight minutes.

But on the day of that record's release, the controversy meter measuring the Pistols rose several significant degrees. A show by the group at the Nashville, next to West Kensington tube station, benefited from the first major article on the group – in *Sounds* by Jonh Ingham – which had appeared two days previously.

　　The venue was packed – Mick Jones, Tony James, Dave Vanian, Adam Ant, and Vic Godard were all there, plus plenty of journalists. Always unpredictable live, however, the Pistols did not play a good show. To liven

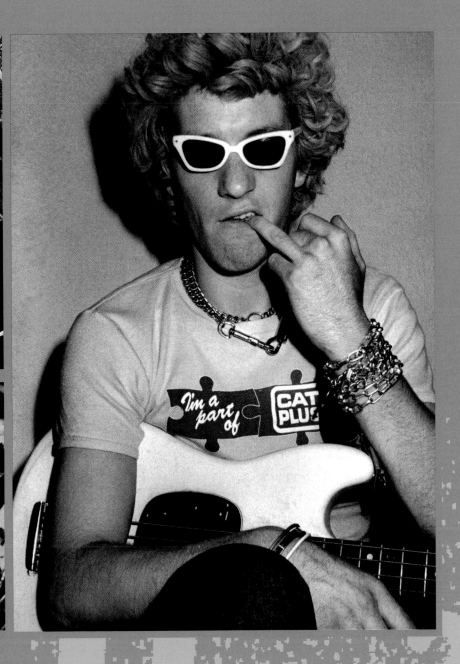

things up, Vivienne Westwood slapped a girl's face right in front of the small stage. In the resultant uproar, both McLaren and Rotten - who had leapt from the stage into the audience - got into a brawl with the girl's boyfriend. In fear, the rest of the audience backed off: it was the strangest thing many of them had ever seen at a supposed 'pop' show, there was no frame of reference whatsoever into which to fit this incident. From now on, violence would be a constant subtext of punk rock. Joe Strummer, as the 101'ers' singer was by now calling himself, studied the group's show, fascinated. Tiring of his constant efforts to keep his own group on the road as some sort of vaguely viable concern, he was impressed not only with the Pistols' show but with the professionalism that he had observed lurking beneath their facade of self-conscious amateurism.

By the next month there was another group out of the ashes of London SS, and therefore peripherally connected to the Pistols: the Heartdrops, comprised of Paul Simonon, Keith Levine, Terry Chimes, and Mick Jones. They were managed by Bernie Rhodes.

Later in the month Joe Strummer was taken by Rhodes to meet them at a squat in Shepherd's Bush. Afterwards, Strummer split from the 101'ers after a show in Haywards Heath; meanwhile, Paul Simonon suggested the Heartdrops be re-named the Clash.

On 16 May, Patti Smith made her UK debut at London's Roundhouse, supported by the Stranglers - the conformist rebel image of the local group was beginning to pay off, though why was their leader Hugh Cornwell, a man with a university degree, masquerading as a naughty schoolboy?

It was London's first punk chic evening, and black leather jackets were out in force. Many of the audience, however, were surprised by the extent of Smith's earnestness; apart from fascinating cultural aberrations like the Ramones, the po-faced atmosphere of college poetry society seemed to permeate much of the New York scene, its key players revealing themselves to the British participants as taking themselves immensely seriously. Didn't the weighty clever-clever irony of, say, Talking Heads seem as though it was coming from musicians more European than the Europeans?

Things were hotting up, not just in the West End of London. In the USA 'X Offender', the debut single from Blondie, was released on Private Stock Records on 15 June 1976.

On 13 July 1976 the first issue of *Sniffin' Glue* was published, the inspiration of an ardent fan from Deptford in South London called Mark Perry. Perry had been inspired to start the fanzine, which he photocopied on a Xerox machine at Oxford Circus tube-station, by an ecstatic Nick Kent review in the *NME* of the Ramones' LP. Soon he would also start his own group, Alternative TV. Fanzines would become a crucial element of the coming change in music.

On 20 July, meanwhile, the Buzzcocks had opened for the Sex Pistols at the Lesser Free Trade Hall in Manchester. Mancunians Pete Shelley and Howard Devoto had been inspired to form their group after seeing the Sex Pistols perform in the city at a previous gig. It was at this northern gig that the Sex Pistols debuted a new song called 'Anarchy in the UK'.

Tony James had initially felt left out in the cold following Mick Jones forming of the Heartdrops. Always resilient, however, he soon found another bunch of musicians with whom to play: the next month saw the birth of Chelsea, consisting of singer Gene October, guitarist Billy Idol and James on bass, as well as drummer John Towe. They were managed by John Krivine, another King's Road creative entrepreneur who ran a shop called Acme Attractions, managed by a dread called Don Letts and Jeanette Lee, a girl from Islington.

That August, meanwhile, saw one of the most significant new developments, one that would bring about a radical change in the British and American music businesses, creating the foundations for independent ('indie') label acts, ultimately creating an entire new genre - one that major record companies eventually managed to skilfully manipulate to their advantage. Stiff Records was founded by Jake Riviera, in partnership with Dave Robinson, former manager of Brinsley Schwartz, with that £400 loan from Dr Feelgood's Lee Brilleaux. It was launched with Nick Lowe's 'So it Goes/Heart of the City'.

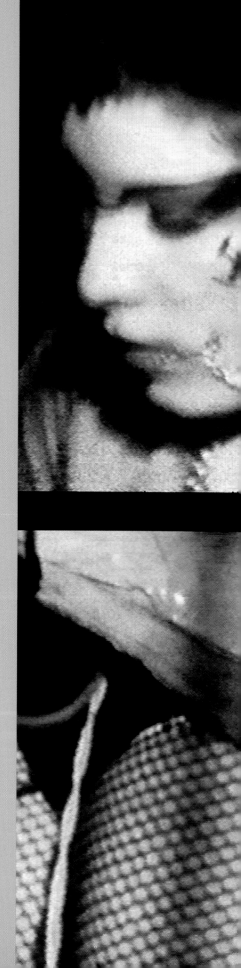

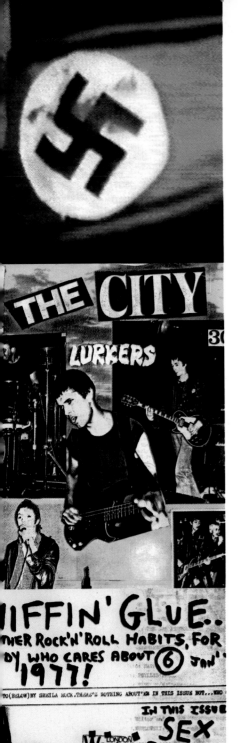

Rotten: 'I'm really shocked at how violent London's become. It's almost beyond belief.'

Pistols fracas at Nashville, reported in the *NME* dated 8 May 1976 by a reader named Neil Tennant, the very same who was to later enjoy fame as a Pet Shop Boy. Some of his report was as follows: 'So how do the Pistols create their atmosphere when their music has failed? By beating up a member of the audience. How else?

'One of their coterie of fag hags picks a fight with the girl sitting next to her. The girl isn't interested but the fag hag succeeds in getting a reaction from her boyfriend. He ain't really an aggressive type, but Ms Hag perseveres...and seven or eight of the band's chums leap over to the scene of the crime from all over the Nashville and proceed to beat the shit out of this bloke. Fists aren't the only weapons.

'Johnny Rotten comes alive.

'While the reaction of the rest of the band is a little confused, Mr Rotten joins in the fight and has a few kicks at the victim. He cackles, he leers, the amps are turned up. He's pleased. The Pistols finish another unforgettable act.'

Rotten: 'Everybody said the Pistols created a lot of violence, but I don't think that's true. Our gigs were probably some of the most peaceful in the world.'

Debbie Harry: 'I want to be a stylist. Certain people are stylists and others mechanists. I really want to do something. We're struggling to find a style and make it a whole personal thing. Like Patti Smith has her whole trip down pat. She has a very masculine and intellectual approach to music and performing. I don't want to do that. Rock and roll is a real masculine business and I think it's time that girls did something in it.'

ADVERTS — LETTS — GORILLAS

43

In the queue one morning in May 1976 at Lisson Grove dole office, Joe Strummer, the singer with the 101'ers, spotted these guys giving him the once-over. 'I thought it was going to be down to a ruck with them when I left the place.' Then Mick Jones came across to talk to him: 'We like you, but we don't like your group.'

'I was just looking for someone to play with, someone I could stir things up with,' said Strummer, whose attitude and approach had changed after his group had been supported by the Sex Pistols at the Nashville. 'And when I met Mick and Paul that day, I recognised that it was what I'd been waiting for. With that gear they had on they just looked right, like a proper group.'

In another version of the story, Strummer ran into Mick Jones, Glen Matlock, and Tony James one Saturday afternoon in Portobello Road, following a 101'ers gig at the Golden Lion. And the same conversation took place. The next day Joe committed himself to the group that was already known as the Clash, making his final appearance with the 101'ers at Clare Halls, Hayward Heath on 5 June 1976.

A few days later Bernie Rhodes, the group's manager, drove him down to a squat in nearby Shepherd's Bush, which Mick Jones shared with Sid Vicious, amongst others. Mick played Joe a love song called 'I'm So Bored With You'. 'I said, "I've got a better idea. Why not call it 'I'm So Bored With The USA'?" And I went off into a corner and wrote some lyrics.'

A month later, on 4 July, the Clash made their stage debut at the Black Swan in Sheffield, supporting the Sex Pistols.

By the time the Clash had set off on the White Riot tour in the spring of 1977, Nicky 'Topper' Headon had joined on drums.

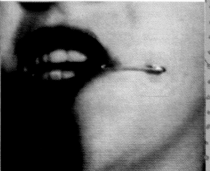

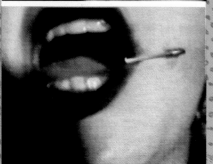

On 21 August, the First European Punk Festival was held in the Mont De Marsan bullring, an hour's drive south of Bordeaux. The brainchild of Skydog Records owner Marc Zermati, it was a good year ahead of its time and only drew a small audience to a bill that included the Damned, Nick Lowe, and local act Little Bob Story. On the coach journey to the gig, Rat Scabies and Nick Lowe had a fight, thereby cementing an invaluble professional relationship that would bear fruit when Lowe produced the Damned's first album.

In the UK this French event drew sizeable press coverage. And the month concluded with a more considered event: on Sunday, 29 August 1976, the Midnight Special show by the Sex Pistols, supported by the Clash and the Buzzcocks, at the Screen on the Green cinema in Islington.

The Clash's first gig had been on Friday, 13 August at Rehearsal Rehearsals, a rundown building in Camden owned by Bernie Rhodes that had become the group's HQ. Giovanni Dadamo reviewed the show in *Sounds*: 'I think they're the first band to come along who'll really frighten the Sex Pistols shitless.' But Charles Shaar Murray, reviewing the Midnight Special show in the *NME*, responded differently to a set plagued by sound problems: the Clash, he wrote, 'are the kind of garage band who should be speedily returned to their garage, preferably with the motor running, which would undoubtedly be more of a loss to their friends and families than to either rock or roll'. These words would come back to haunt him. In fact, in the great tradition of support bands being stitched up by the main act, the quality of the Clash's sound was nowhere near that of the Pistols: throughout his first tenure with the group, Bernie Rhodes seemed to almost encourage the Clash to have an atrocious live sound, attempting somehow to turn this into some kind of perverse virtue.

Dave Robinson, who co-founded Stiff Records with Jake Riviera

Tony James: 'I was looking for people to play with, so I answered an ad in Melody Maker for a guitar-player. I drove down to Bromley. There was Billy Idol there, Siouxsie Sioux, and some other bloke. I told him I couldn't play guitar, but I could play bass. So Billy said, "That's alright." We rehearsed a bit, but nothing really happened. Then we both separately answered an ad placed by John Krivine. It was to back Gene October."

46

babylon burning

Notting Hill had become mythologised in the British consciousness in 1958, when it had been riven by racist attacks by Teddy Boys on the area's new inhabitants, immigrants from what lingered of the British colonies in the Caribbean. It was in this area that the first shebeens sprang up, illegal after-hours drinking dens aimed at and run by West Indians, which were also popular with bohemian whites – Christine Keeler, for example, the 'goodtime' girl whose relationship with Conservative Foreign Minister John Profumo was to bring down the Tory government, ushering in Harold Wilson's Labour government and the Swinging Sixties.

By the end of the 1960s Notting Hill was Britain's hotbed of artistic anarchy. Its tall Victorian houses divided into rabbit warrens of one-room bedsits, the area was the British equivalent of San Francisco's Haight-Ashbury. Here flourished drug dealing, the underground press and musicianship of an especially 'alternative' nature.

In 1970 the area's traditional militancy received a focus for protest following the opening of the Westway, a stretch of overhead motorway linking the area with London's West End that was the first American-style inner city freeway in the capital; the construction of the Westway, adjacent to the top floors of Notting Hill's houses, had led to severe disruption in the quality of life of those dwelling nearby.

'The Sound of The Westway', the mantle the Clash shrewdly took upon themselves, was a strong concept. Tying in acts to their particular locale never caused anyone any harm, whether it was Liverpool, Asbury Park or Trenchtown. And the romance of quasi-bohemian Notting Hill only added further spice.

The annual carnival took place at the end of August, on the Sunday and Bank Holiday Monday. It drew up to a million visitors every year, eager to watch the spectacular, shimmering floats and sway to the sound systems, playing music from not only the carnival's original home of Trinidad but also - increasingly - from Jamaica.

In 1976 the event that became known as the Notting Hill Carnival Riot occurred around five o'clock in the afternoon of the second day. Under the Westway, and along the length of Ladbroke Grove black youths rioted, in fierce battle with the police. Joe Strummer, Paul Simonon and Bernie Rhodes found themselves in the epicentre of the riot. This was the incident that led to Joe Strummer and Mick Jones writing 'White Riot'.

A few days later, on 5 September, the Clash played the Roundhouse, first on the bill at a show topped by the Kursaal Flyers, a Southend group who'd had some chart success - and who were precisely the kind of middle-of-the-second-division group about to be swept away once and for all by the coming tidal wave of musical change.

Opening the show to the regular Sunday night audience of post-hippie teenagers, still sitting cross-legged on the floor as though they were watching Yes, Joe Strummer felt obliged to deliver his State of the Union message: 'I've been trying to go out recently, but I've had to stay in. And the only thing I've got at home is a TV that hasn't got any sound on it. So I'm staying in, right, and I just want to hear sounds, I don't want to see no visuals, I want to go out and see some groups. But there ain't anything to go out and see. I've seen it all before. So I have to stay at home and watch TV without sound and lip-read my way through it. I'd just like to protest about this state of affairs. So if there's any of you people in the audience who aren't past it yet, and if you can do anything, why don't you get up and do it, instead of, like, lying around?'

In the annals of punk, this was considered the first articulation of what was to become known as its Do-It-Yourself ethic.

Later in the month a larger version of this spirit was due to be manifested. Realising the need to focus assorted disparate energies, Malcolm McLaren had arranged for the 100 Club, an adventurous venue on London's Oxford Street, to host the Punk Festival, on 20 and 21 September. It was the kind of vaguely elitist 'event' that pop group managers from now on would consistently manipulate to promote their acts. Day one was to feature the Sex Pistols, the Clash, Subway Sect, Siouxsie and the Banshees, and Stinky Toys, who ended up opening the second night.

During the Clash's set, Mick Jones broke a string; sticking a cheap transistor radio up to the mike, Joe Strummer tuned into an item about the civil war in northern Ireland. The synchronicity stuck, and such audio *objets trouvé* became part of the mix of the Clash.

Other acts performing on day two were the Damned, the Vibrators, and the Buzzcocks. But the most significant impact of the second night came not from the onstage 'musicians', but from a member of the audience. One Sid Vicious (aka John Ritchie), a close friend of John 'Johnny Rotten' Lydon, was arrested after a beer glass was thrown and a girl's eye damaged. When Caroline Coon, the *Melody Maker* journalist who had founded the drugs-bust legal charity Release, remonstrated with the police that it wasn't Sid who'd done it, she was also arrested.

Siouxsie and the Banshees; (left to right) John McKay, Steve Severin, Kenny Morris and Siouxsie Sioux.

Part of Sid's extremely variable reputation was due to his having allegedly invented a dance called the Pogo; Sid, however, was unaware that he had invented this dance as all he was doing was bouncing on his feet to see the group onstage. Sid had performed the previous night, playing drums with Siouxsie and the Banshees. Billy Idol, from the same area of Bromley in south-east London as Siouxsie, had been scheduled to play with them, but told the group he was too committed to Chelsea. Siouxsie and the Banshees performed one number, 'The Lord's Prayer', lasting over twenty minutes.

As a showcase for the Sex Pistols, the 100 Club event – which was unquestionably a watershed – certainly had an effect. It got the group that first music paper front cover, for example, in the *NME*, shared with Dr Feelgood, as though the paper was hedging its bets about the future. (A surely apocryphal story later had the end-of-year *NME* poll fixed to bring in the Pistols as Best New Group after the readers again had voted overwhelmingly for the purgatorial likes of Genesis offshoot Brand X. Who would believe such a tale?)

On 28 September, McLaren had a meeting with Nick Mobbs, an A & R man at EMI Records. On 9 October 1976, the Sex Pistols signed to the label. 'For me,' said Mobbs, 'the Sex Pistols are a backlash against the "nice little band" syndrome and the general stagnation of the music industry. They've got to happen for all our sakes.' The next day the Pistols were in Lansdowne studios with Dave Goodman. When the sessions failed to gel, they changed studios and producers. By 17 October, they were in Wessex Studios, working with producer Chris Thomas.

A week later 'New Rose', the Damned's first single, was released on Stiff.

And on Saturday, 23 October, the Clash headlined a show at London's Institute for Contemporary Arts. Also on the bill were Subway Sect and Snatch, featuring Judy Nylon and Patti Paladin. Halfway through the Clash's set, however, love play between Shane McGowan and his girlfriend took a cannibalistic turn: Shane, who was in the process of forming his group the Nipple Erectors, was having his right earlobe nibbled when he felt a searing pain as it was bitten off. Newspaper reports of this bizarre incident only fuelled the controversy about punk rock. What on earth was it drawing out of the nation's psyche?

That afternoon, as the Clash had hung out near the ICA before going down there for a soundcheck, they had experienced another significant first sighting in the annals of punk: a group from Surrey called the Jam had set up their equipment near Chinatown in Soho Market next to the Rock On Records stall and, wearing their Mod suits, played a short set. The result? Publicity in both *Sounds* and *Melody Maker*.

The next Friday the Clash played again, at Fulham Town Hall, sandwiched between opening act the Vibrators and Roogalator. It felt as though you were in the presence of an ongoing piece of art, as intuitive as the work of Jackson Pollock, a great inspiration on the part of Paul Simonon who had devised the paint-bespattered clothes and shoes that

Brian James: 'With bands like it's the attitude that's importa Kids come and see us and th think, hey, that could be me up that stage, I could be as good that if I tried. So maybe they b their first guitar.'

Paul Simonon on his years Holland Park's exclusive Bya Shaw Art College, which attended on a scholarship: was really good there. All th other kids had really ri parents, so you could just ni their canvas and paints a they'd get their fathers to b them replacements.'

Left: *Siouxsie Sioux.*
Below: *Tony James and Billy Idol in Chelsea.*

Tony James: 'London was a cultural desert. It was hard to even buy a leather jacket, and virtually impossible to buy Bob Dylan sunglasses. In Paris you could get all this stuff. There was this scene there built around Little Bob Story and Skydog Records.'

the group wore onstage that night. Onstage they lived up to Mick Jones's original, most innocent dreams for the group: that they should be a blur of oustanding visuals in which the sound that came offstage could be almost irrelevant. 'All I wanted at first was that we should look really fantastic.' During the Clash's set the crowd surged forwards to watch them: when the group came offstage the audience evaporated. 'Even then,' said Mick Jones, 'people knew about us and were coming just to see us - it was building as early as that.'

Things moved right along that month. Eddie And The Hot Rods, whose Marquee show eight months before the Sex Pistols had so successfully trashed, hit the Top Forty with 'Teenage Depression'. Working with ace session guitarist and proud wearer of black leather trousers Chris Spedding, once a member of the Sharks, an influence on Mick Jones, were the Vibrators; they released a single called Pogo Dancing. Later the same week in November they put out another single without Spedding, 'We Vibrate'.

In New York Richard Hell and the Voidoids were also beginning to play, debuting at CBGBs on 18 November . In Britain Hell had already had a single released by Stiff; 'Blank Generation' (*I'm a part of the Blank Generation/I can take it or leave it anytime*) in a limited edition of 5,000.

Meanwhile, Chelsea supported the Stranglers at the Nashville on 21 November. Afterwards Billy Idol, Tony James and John Towe defected en masse from singer Gene October and formed Generation X, named after a vox pop book about Mod culture in the early 1960s.

Tony James: 'Punk rock seems like my childhood, the glorious, very exciting naivete of rock'n'roll. Stenguns and guitars seem very idealistic when you're twenty. I'm sure the record company people decided that that was the handle they should sell it on. But it was the first time that rock'n'roll bit the hand that fed it.'

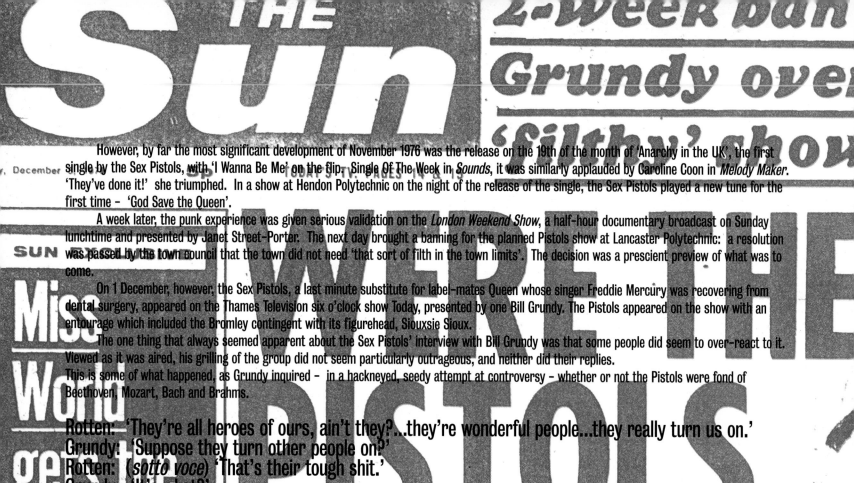

However, by far the most significant development of November 1976 was the release on the 19th of the month of 'Anarchy in the UK', the first single by the Sex Pistols, with 'I Wanna Be Me' on the flip. Single Of The Week in *Sounds*, it was similarly applauded by Caroline Coon in *Melody Maker*. 'They've done it!' she triumphed. In a show at Hendon Polytechnic on the night of the release of the single, the Sex Pistols played a new tune for the first time – 'God Save the Queen'.

A week later, the punk experience was given serious validation on the *London Weekend Show*, a half-hour documentary broadcast on Sunday lunchtime and presented by Janet Street-Porter. The next day brought a banning for the planned Pistols show at Lancaster Polytechnic: a resolution was passed by the town council that the town did not need 'that sort of filth in the town limits'. The decision was a prescient preview of what was to come.

On 1 December, however, the Sex Pistols, a last minute substitute for label-mates Queen whose singer Freddie Mercury was recovering from dental surgery, appeared on the Thames Television six o'clock show Today, presented by one Bill Grundy. The Pistols appeared on the show with an entourage which included the Bromley contingent with its figurehead, Siouxsie Sioux.

The one thing that always seemed apparent about the Sex Pistols' interview with Bill Grundy was that some people did seem to over-react to it. Viewed as it was aired, his grilling of the group did not seem particularly outrageous, and neither did their replies.

This is some of what happened, as Grundy inquired – in a hackneyed, seedy attempt at controversy – whether or not the Pistols were fond of Beethoven, Mozart, Bach and Brahms.

Rotten: 'They're all heroes of ours, ain't they?...they're wonderful people...they really turn us on.'
Grundy: 'Suppose they turn other people on?'
Rotten: (*sotto voce*) 'That's their tough shit.'
Grundy: 'It's what?'
Rotten: 'Nothing. A rude word. Next question.'
Grundy: 'No, no, what was the rude word?'
Rotten: 'Shit.'
Grundy: 'Was it really? Good heavens, you frightened me to death.'
Rotten: 'Oh alright Siegfried.'

After bantering in a bored manner with Siouxsie, Grundy then suggested that perhaps he might meet her after the show – however, there was clearly no intention on his part of doing so, it was just a glib TV presenter's throwaway line. 'You dirty sod. You dirty old man,' laughed Steve Jones.
Grundy: 'Well, keep going chief, keep going. Go on, you've got another ten seconds. Say something outrageous.'

Jones: 'You dirty bastard.'
Grundy: 'Go on, again.'
Jones: 'You dirty fucker.'
Grundy: 'What a clever boy.'
Jones: 'You fucking rotter.'

The next day the story of the Sex Pistols interview by Bill Grundy was on the front page of every British newspaper. 'The filth and the fury' trumpeted

54

s the money rolls in, rock
oup faces tour ban and
V chiefs suspend Grundy

THE GROUP, from left, Glen Matlock...

PUNK? CALL IT FILTHY LUCRE

By Garth Pearce and Patrick Clancy

CONCERTS for the Sex Pistols were cancelled and interviewer Bill Grundy was suspended last night in a row over the group's four-letter outburst on TV.

But the real four-letter word behind it was CASH. For E.M.I., Britain's biggest record company, has a big financial interest in the "punk rock" men.

The firm's records chief, Mr. Leslie Hill, thought the four words were "coarse and outrageous" and swear at Grundy on the Thames "Today" programme—said, to said there was no question of dropping their contract.

Another official admitted "After all it was anyone's guess how big they could be." But it was denied the incident was a publicity stunt.

Yet the rewards are enormous. If, as the result of the group's behaviour, a record made the Pop Ten it would sell 10,000 copies a day and gross 130,000 a week, with the company clearing two per cent on every single.

The build-up

The Sex Pistols, led by a one-time sewage worker who styles himself Johnny Rotten, were launched last April by Malcolm McLaren, 29-year-old owner of a London clothes shop called "Sex."

Rotten—real name Lydon—and Glen Matlock, Steve Jones, and Paul Cook, are all 20 years old and were unemployed before. Mr. McLaren gave them guitars and billed them as leaders of the new rage. Punk Rock.

in
t of

ren

sonal

Page 10

Kong and I
love at first—

t Cartoon
rt Lancaster

 case remember
that we have
for thinking
Herald Angels
n rock group

ie hit by mutiny but—

mebody

THE SUN, Friday, December 3, 1976

The Great Punk Rock Storm

'I DID IT TO SHOW THEY ARE JUST FOUL MOUTHED YOBS'

Grundy slams back at critics

BY KEITH DEVES

TV interviewer Bill Grundy yesterday defended his behaviour on the Today show, when a Punk Rock group used four-letter obscenities that shocked thousands of viewers.

Punk Rock is the craziest pop cult of them all

What the Sun said on October 15.   Bill Grundy in London yesterday.

Way out and wild ... the controversial Sex Pistols with some of their fans

THESE HYPOCRITES, BY A POP MUM

BY MICHAEL GAY

Winfield 'pop-up' ice cube trays. All it takes is a twist.

49p the twin p
Wonderful Value. Great Qual

55

Cancelled

The night of the Bill Grundy show, the Heartbeakers arrived at London airport, ready to support the Pistols as part of the Anarchy tour.

Tony James: 'Nowadays seven-year olds talk like that when they go down the local newsagents.'

Shortly after the Bill Grundy fiasco, Radio Luxembourg's top DJ Tony Prince was suspended for two days for refusing to pre-record an interview with the Sex Pistols.

Simone Thomas: 'I was sixteen at the time. My life revolved around David Bowie and Roxy Music and dressing up and going to gigs. I'd met Siouxsie at a Roxy concert. She was from the same part of London as me and she started going out with Steve Severin, who was part of the same scene. Berlin was also a very good friend of mine who used to have really good parties. We all went to the 100 Club together to watch Siouxsie. We also used to go to Louise's, a lesbian club in Soho which had a room upstairs on the entrance floor where you could sit and talk. We used to talk a lot because we were all speeding at the time – everyone was.'

Simone Thomas: 'We became known as the Bromley contingent after the Pistols played at Orpington College and they came to one of Berlin's parties. We were the first fans - in fact, I wasn't really a fan, but I just went along with it. I remember Malcolm paid us to come to the airport when they went to Holland so it looked as though they had a lot of fans.

'I felt I was in a movie and just wore the clothes to fit my image. But inside I didn't feel the part. I'm sure a lot of people felt like that.

'One afternoon Siouxsie called and asked if I'd like to be on TV. We were picked up in a chauffeur-driven Mercedes with Thames Television written on the back window. When we arrived at the studio, Malcolm and Vivienne were already there with the Pistols. We were given loads of drinks, and then they went straight on air. Malcolm was trying to get them to be wild and outrageous: I was hoping my dad wouldn't be watching and I sat there with an imbecilic grin.

'I think people wanted to get angry: the man who kicked in his TV set was obviously an idiot. By present standards it was incredibly tame. Bill Grundy was like a child himself - he wasn't wise at all, he should have defused the situation.

'Malcolm got what he wanted. The Sex Pistols was Malcolm's baby and the boys went along with it.

'For a couple of months after they'd played the 100 Club I was in the Banshees - I used to play classical violin. Sid would be there at rehearsals, doing weird things with razors to himself and drinking tequila. The Sex Pistols, including Johnny Rotten, just seemed to be after whatever they could get for themselves. In fact, Johnny Rotten was obnoxious, like a little boy, with his rat face, thinking every word he said was that of God - I didn't think very much to him at all. Steve Jones thought he could get into the pants of any girl. Glen was intelligent and quiet. And Paul was sweet and naive. I didn't feel able to talk to Malcolm, although Vivienne seemed more sensitive.'

the headline in the *Daily Mirror*, whose entire front page was given over to the story, including an account of the Essex truck driver who had kicked in the screen of his television set: 'Lorry-driver James Holmes, 47, was so outraged that his eight-year-old son Lee heard the swearing that he kicked in the screen of his TV.'

From now on the media obsession with the Sex Pistols never went away - they were to remain on the front pages of the tabloids for the next week. The commercial life of punk rock had been kickstarted by what was in reality a rather petty and insignificant piece of outrage. But this was really a manifestation of a declining, post-colonial nation in a state of terminal identity confusion.

By 7 December Sir John Read, the chairman of EMI Records, was obliged to comment on the 'incident' at the EMI Annual General Meeting: 'The Sex Pistols incident, which started with a disgraceful interview given by this young pop group on Thames TV last week...the Sex Pistols have acquired a reputation for aggressive behaviour which they certainly demonstrated in public. There is no excuse for this...I need hardly add we shall do everything we can to restrain their public behaviour...Our view within EMI is that we should seek to discourage records that are likely to give offence to the majority of the people...EMI should not set itself up as a public censor, (but it does) seek to encourage restraint.'

Clearly the future of the Pistols with EMI was in jeopardy. 'Whether EMI does release any more of the group's records will have to be carefully considered,' added Read. 'I need hardly add that we shall do everything we can to restrain their public behaviour, although this is a matter over which we had no real control.'

Elsewhere the Pistols were already running the full gamut of another sort of Establishment pressure - the night of Read's speech, the group had been scheduled to play in Bournemouth, but the show was cancelled. In fact, a full tour by the Sex Pistols, the Clash, the Damned and the Heartbreakers had been booked to run throughout December. When they arrived at the University of East Anglia in Norwich for the first date on 3 December, the acts discovered that the gig had been banned by the university's vice chancellor - furious students had arranged a sit-in to protest against the decision. Six other dates were cancelled almost immediately. A curious pastiche of Ken Kesey's hippie Magic Bus trips was enacted as the groups were driven the length and breadth of England and Wales, looking for gigs that hadn't been cancelled, staying in expensive hotels. All the while, they were being bankrolled by EMI.

When they did get to play - in Leeds, Manchester, Caerphilly, Plymouth - the group would be covered in a barrage of spit and beer: appreciative 'gobbing' made a good excuse for the dirty-needle-induced doses of

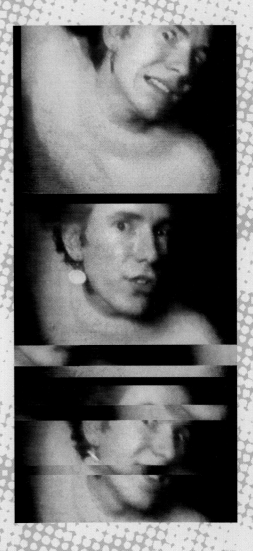

hepatitis - usually from shooting up speed, not necessarily heroin - with which several key players would be hospitalised.

The Sex Pistols spent the Christmas and New Year's Day holidays in a state of considerable anticipation: did they still have a record deal?

If the Grundy interview and its aftermath had left the future uncertain for the Sex Pistols (although in Christmas week 'Anarchy in the UK' entered the *NME* chart for one week at number 27 and altogether sold 55,000 records), it had simultaneously signalled a clear path forward for punk rock as a whole.

On 21 December, a new club, the Roxy in Neal Street, Covent Garden, saw the first performance by Generation X. Siouxsie and the Banshees were the support act.

The Roxy, which would only last in that precise form for 100 days, became briefly the punk Mecca. Located in a former gay club called Chaugerama's, it was opened by Andy Czezowski, at that time the manager of Generation X. He was also the accountant for Acme Attractions, the only rival to Sex on the King's Road. Acme Attractions sold original American clothes from the 1950s, the source material of much of what was designed by Vivienne Westwood for Sex. Running the shop for John Krivine, its owner, were Jeanette Lee and Don Letts, a young Rastafarian who had been profoundly influenced by the message of Bob Marley.

When Czezowski opened the Roxy, he asked Letts to be the DJ. Letts in turn co-opted his brother Desmond and friend Leo Williams to run the two bars, one upstairs and one in the basement. The venue was tiny: upstairs there was a small hanging-out area; the stage was downstairs, in the low-ceilinged room whose roof was frequently fractured by guitar necks; the DJ booth was next to the stage. Leo Williams worked the downstairs bar, where the most popular drinks were Colt 45 and Special Brew, the angel dust of lagers; he and the Letts brothers also sold sno-cone spliffs.

The ganja helped establish a cross-cultural mood underpinned by the soundtrack of roots reggae that Don Letts would play in between the amphetamine charge of the punk acts booked for each night. 'There weren't enough punk records to play,' remembered Letts, 'so I just brought my reggae collection along.'

At the time reggae was considered by a select few to be the only interesting music around. As a consequence of Letts' record choices, he helped set in motion the celebrated punk-reggae fusion which would find its most ardent interpretations in the music of the Clash and be celebrated later in the year in Bob Marley's 'Punky Reggae Party'.

ANARCHY IN THE U.K.

Leo Williams: 'The Roxy was a complete eye-opener for me – it was obvious the times needed a change, and the rock business specifically needed to change. I used to work in an engineering factory. But one day I worked out exactly how long it would take me to get anywhere financially on my wages... and I realised it would take a very long time. So I was starting to think of becoming a musician.

'When Don started playing reggae at the Roxy, Andy just let him get on with it. After we started filming, we'd go back to Forest Hill, where we were living, sharing a place with Chrissie Hynde, and Don would start editing his footage together with cellotape. All the groups would come back to our place after the Roxy. Everyone was doing things like *Sniffin' Glue*, and it taught me you could do things for yourself.

'John Lydon would be down there a lot, as was Sid. John would sometimes pick on people, but Sid was a really cool guy.

'Although they played there on New Year's Day, 1977, the Clash weren't really part of the Roxy trip. People like the Buzzcocks, Siouxsie and the Damned were much more so. I remember when Eater had a pig's head onstage one night. Their drummer, Dee Generate, was a wicked player: his mother would always be down there. The Heartbreakers were always down there, always out of it, drunk as well as smacked. The Jam, though, were always the best act that played there – really kicking. The place used to be so sweaty down there.

'It wasn't a money venture for Andy. He was just the one who had to do it at that time. He just wanted to get things happening.

'Then me and Don started managing the Slits, up and down the motorway, with Nora, Ari Upp's mother. Ari was a pain at first when she started coming down the Roxy: she must have been thirteen or fourteen. She didn't give a shit and had a lot of front from day one. We'd take Strummer to places like the 4 Aces in Dalston, and to Hammersmith Palais – after one show he wrote "White Man" in Hammersmith Palais.

'Everyone was doing speed – the Adverts used to do masses, for example, particularly Gaye Advert – but there was smack around as well. One night I did some by mistake with Keith Levene – I thought it was coke.

'After the Roxy closed, the Vortex opened in Wardour Street. The atmosphere there was always slightly heavy, with hooligans disguised as bouncers.

'I can't remember seeing Malcolm down the Roxy, although Bernie was often there. Sebastian Conran was often there as well: the Clash used to live in his house in Regents Park and pretend it was a squat. But it was obvious the scene was totally changing: kids were getting involved because it was a breath of fresh air.'

Bernie Rhodes on the Anarchy tour: 'Kids should have the chance to see the entertainment they want. The Government tells them to work hard for their money and get the nation back on its feet and then they won't give them the chance to see the entertainment they want.'

Jerry Nolan: 'The English bands are supposed to hate everything. But those kids care so much – they care about their music, the fucked-up state of their country, the kids who come to see them – they care so much it's ridiculous.'

Tony James: 'Andy Czezowski and John Krivine told us there was this heavy gangster gay bar we could get a gig at. I remember building the stage with Derwood, John Towe, and Billy.'

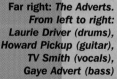

Far right: The Adverts. From left to right: Laurie Driver (drums), Howard Pickup (guitar), TV Smith (vocals), Gaye Advert (bass)

Top: Eater, featuring Dee Generate (13), the youngest drummer in Punk.

*Mr & Mrs Nora Rotten,
mother of Ari Upp, singer
with the Slits.
Nepotism Rools OK?*

61

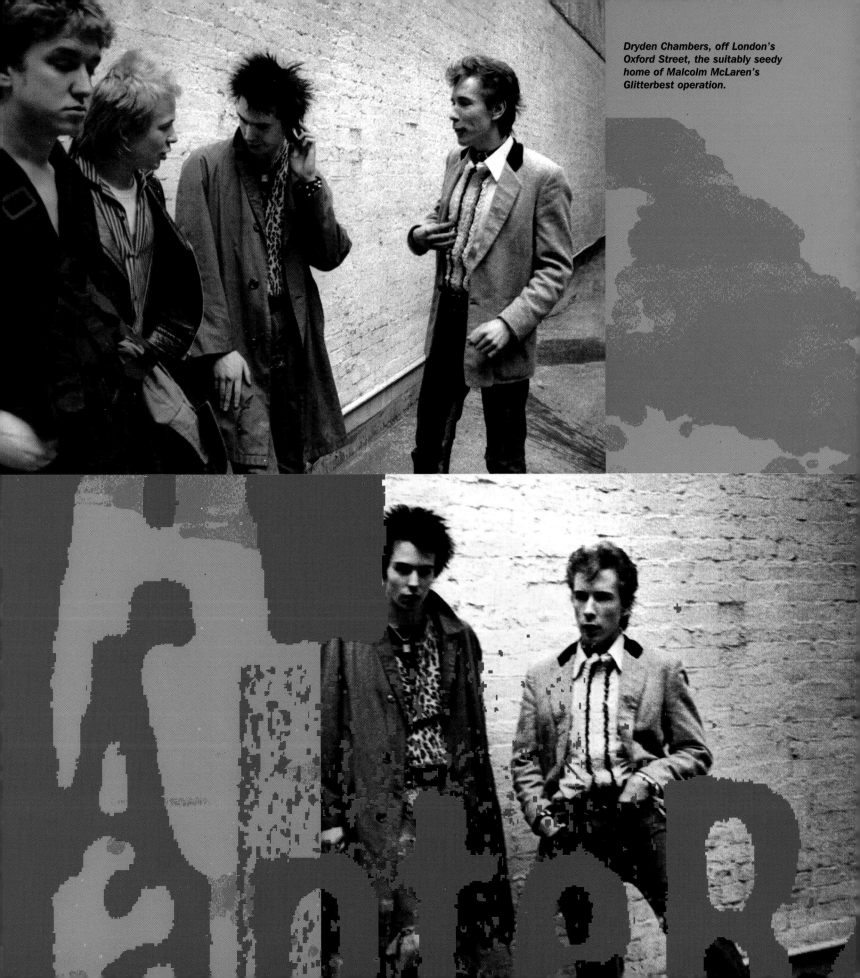

Dryden Chambers, off London's Oxford Street, the suitably seedy home of Malcolm McLaren's Glitterbest operation.

...close to Weaver studios where the Plaza's car, he required two stitches in his arm, & le...

5

everybody wa... squeezed int...

"I really like NEW YORK.

...the kind of place...

As 1976 juddered its three-chord trick into 1977, there were those aware of the apocalyptic predictions for the year. Especially those with any awareness of reggae culture. In his attempts at co-opting the role of sole punk archetype for himself, John 'Rotten' Lydon has attempted to claim that he was the first person to play reggae on the radio in the UK – in a Capital Radio show broadcast on 16 July 1977. In fact, both Capital and Radio London had their own regular reggae programmes, aimed at London's Jamaican immigrant population.

In his autobiography, Rotten made a claim of extraordinary self-delusion: '..suddenly you'd get Joe Strummer and the Clash say, "We always loved reggae." But those fucks never did. They were not brought up with it the same way I was.' This, of course, is arrogant nonsense - certainly Mick Jones and Paul Simonon had been brought up in similar areas to himself, where the sound of reggae sailing out of windows was the norm. His comment is also a good example of the almost complete lack of solidarity between punk acts, all of whom seemed only too eager to slag off their rivals endlessly. What is far more extraordinary is that Lydon was still persisting with this level of self-delusion sixteen years later.

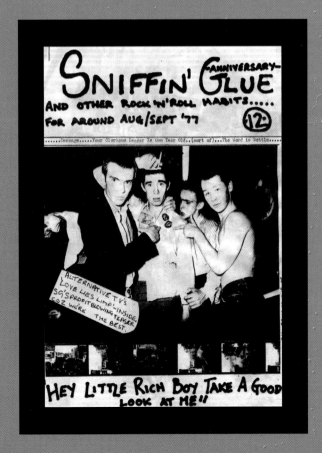

If I seem a little jittery,
I can't restrain myself,
I'm falling into fancy fragments,
Can't contain myself,
I gotta breakdown, breakdown yeah

I can stand austerity,
But it gets a little much,
When there's all these livid things,
That you never get to touch,
I gotta breakdown, breakdown yeah.
   - Breakdown, Howard Devoto

Reggae was as much at the musical cutting edge as punk music. People looking for something new and exciting were automatically drawn to the two styles - they were what was around. And, to the punk fan at least, the two forms fed each other - the cultural borrowing from reggae to punk was largely not reciprocated, however. All the same, invaluable and pungent reggae or Rastafarian terms and concepts like 'Babylon' and 'heavy manners', became part of the cultural fabric of, first, punks and then all white inner-city youth.

A reggae anthem of the time, 'Two Sevens Clash' by the appropriately named Culture, the biggest-selling record in Jamaica in 1976, announced the numerological significance of the year 1977, a harbinger of colossal change for followers of Rastafari. The Clash stated it more simply: '*No Elvis, Beatles, or Rolling Stones/in 1977*...And in August of that year Elvis Presley, the king - the inventor, some would claim - of rock'n'roll, died on his Memphis toilet seat...*WHAT ON EARTH HAD BEEN UNLEASHED?* The world became divided into those who understood and those who didn't.

There are even those mystics who claim that this was the time when the battle against Babylon was won; and that subsequent chaos, such as the war in Yugoslavia, is a dreadfully necessary cleaning out of the dirt in the collective unconscious.

Whatever, punk was snowballing. At the very end of 1976, on 28 December, the Buzzcocks became the first punk band to have a record out on their own label, New Hormones, thereby setting in motion the garden shed D-I-Y punk ethic. The record was an EP, entitled 'Spiral Scratch', consisting of four tracks: 'Breakdown', 'Time's Up', 'Boredom' and 'Friends Of Mine'. Formed by guitarist Pete Shelley and vocalist Howard Devoto after they had seen the first Manchester gig by the Pistols, the Buzzcocks were completed by bassist Steve Diggle and drummer John Maher. 'This group *is* the new-wave,' wrote Mark P in *Sniffin' Glue*.

Meanwhile, Stiff Records signed the Adverts, a four-piece led by TV Smith and Gaye Advert, art students from Torquay who had been inspired by seeing the Pistols and moved to London to form a group. The amphetamine-sputtering 'One Chord Wonders' was their first release.

As for the Sex Pistols themselves, however, matters now seemed to be running almost out of control. On 4 January 1977, the group breezed through London's Heathrow airport, on their way to Amsterdam for a five-day Dutch tour. During their course through the airport, they were reported to have spat, sworn and vomited as they checked in for their flight. This story, faithfully reported in the British press, was fabricated for their benefit by Malcolm McLaren. In fact, the group had been running so late that an EMI representative ensured that they bypassed the KLM check-in desk and went straight to the plane.

Like a child ceaselessly crying wolf for its own dysfunctional reasons, McLaren had gone too far. Two days later, citing this airport incident as being the last straw, Sir John Read threw the group off the label. 'The Sex Pistols have acquired a reputation for aggressive behaviour which they have certainly demonstrated in public.'

Above: Buzzcocks, from left to right: Steve Diggle (guitar), John Maher (drums), Steve Garvey (bass), Pete Shelley (guitar/vocals). The most successful punk group from outside London, their first gig posters were printed on the pages of tabloid newspapers. After just eleven shows, founder member Howard Devoto left to form the moderately successful, more idiosyncratic Magazine (below).

On 9 January 1977 McLaren had a meeting with Derek Green, the feisty managing director of A&M Records.   However, it was nearly another three weeks before the Sex Pistols and EMI came to a final settlement, on 28 January, whereby the group were paid £50,000 to leave the label.

In New York, meanwhile, Talking Heads were now one of the biggest new groups, drawing packed audiences at CBGBs, and readying songs for a prospective album.
      On 25 January 1977, 'The Ramones Leave Home', the group's second album, was released. Such speed of production certainly seemed to accord with the punk spirit; for the rest of 1977 one of the most notable aspects was the rapidity with which events and releases moved.
      Two days later, on 27 January , the Clash signed to CBS. It was a record deal at the time for a punk group - £100,000 for six albums. A major commitment to an apparent musical fad from such a multinational giant. Within the D-I-Y context of the Buzzcocks releasing 'Spiral Scratch' on their own label, however, it drew the Clash into constant purist scrutiny about their 'motivation'. *Sniffin' Glue* was especially sniffy. Even the group themselves were rapidly to be disabused of their belief in CBS's assurances to have given them complete artistic control.

From now on, things seemed really to speed up, including every possible manner of controversy.
      The Sunday after the Clash signed to CBS, for example, the Stranglers played the Rainbow, supporting the Climax Blues Band. Hugh Cornwell, the group's singer and principal songwriter, was always one to court controversy aggressively: that night he wittily chose to wear a T-shirt on which a logo for the Ford motor company had had the car manufacturer's name transmogrify into the word 'Fuck'. *Wow: what a heavy rebel!!!* What was it like to be still in the Third Form? Of such revolutionary acts was punk composed. A predictable brouhaha erupted until the Rainbow's management pulled the plugs, forcing Cornwell off the stage - no doubt as he had desired.
      Early in February Stiff Records made a licensing deal with Island Records to distribute Jake Riviera and Dave Robinson's label for all markets in the world, except the USA. A new single and album from the Damned were imminent, released on 18 February , after having been recorded in ten days. 'Neat Neat Neat' was a classic of ramalama 180mph punk rock, a trailer for 'Damned Damned Damned', their album, produced by Nick Lowe. The LP similarly consisted of short, sharp songs played extremely fast. The first of Britain's punk groups to be out of the starting-gate with an album, this also was in many ways the zenith of the Damned's career. 'When we signed to Stiff,' Rat Scabies said later, 'they said, "Do you want to be rich or do you want to be famous?" We said, "famous", because we thought if we were famous we must be rich as well.....'

 Although thus securely lodged into the annals of punk, the origins of Stiff really lay in pub rock. It was ironic then that the label should serve as the template for dozens of subsequent punk singles labels, as well as the entire 'indie' genre.
      That month Blondie released its eponymously titled first album on Private Stock. The group's punchy, melodic songs owed as much to girl groups of the previous decade as to the New York New Wave, as this movement was already sometimes becoming known.
      On 12 February 1977, meanwhile, a new unknown group called the Police went into Pathway studio in Islington to cut a single, for a total of £150, before they played their first gig. The record was called 'Fall Out/Nothing Achieving', both sides written by Stewart Copeland, formerly the drummer with Curved Air. The other members of the group were guitarist Henry Padovani and a singer and bass-player from Newcastle called Sting. With considerable reluctance, Stewart's brother Miles was persuaded to put the single out on his own Illegal Records. On 3 March Cherry Vanilla, Johnny Thunders And The Heartbreakers and the Police started a tour with a date at the Roxy; the Police doubled as Vanilla's backing group. Once David Bowie's press agent, Cherry Vanilla wrote and sang 'erotic' songs.
      Also in February Snatch, the group formed by Judy Nylon and Patti Paladin, two of those women in black leather with foreign accents Chris Thomas had noted, had their first single out: 'IRT/Stanley', on Bomp records.

Much less marginally, on 25 February the Jam – hits of the Roxy – signed to Polydor for £6,000, substantially renegotiating the deal three months later. Before they split in October 1982, they would have had sixteen songs in the UK Top Forty, with four songs at number one. Their sudden signing to Polygram was an act of near-panic by Polydor A&R man Chris Parry, who had missed both the Pistols and the Clash, and who had now heard that the Jam were about to sign to pub rock label Chiswick.

Three days later an act called Johnny Moped opened for the Damned at the Roxy. The group was made up of Fred Berk on drums, Dave Berk on bass and Johnny Moped on vocals, with Xerexes on sax and a guitarist called Sissy Bar. 'Sissy Bar' was in fact Chrissie Hynde, who briefly joined the group as second guitarist.

Meanwhile, more punk controversy was raising its noisy head. At the beginning of March the Ramones were in conflict with their record

David Byrne: 'In terms of the lyrics, I wanted to strip everything down to the level of it being nothing more than what one hears in a conversation. I felt lyrics were becoming long-winded and pointless, that they needed to be far more to the point.'

Mick Jones: 'I was so into speed, I don't even recall making the first album.'

David Byrne: 'One thing I thought was that us, along with a lot of other new groups, are very self-aware: about where they perform, what they look like, how they appear to the press... very aware of every move they make and what the supposed ramifications will be. It could seem very contrived but I think that's the way people are now. The days of naive, primitive rock bands are gone.'

David Byrne: 'Rock just isn't something that wells out of the street anymore. The punk thing was a very self-aware reaction and in that sense it's very historically oriented. Part of its meaning and importance comes out of that historical perspective. Without that I don't think it would have seemed that important at all.'

On 17 January 1977, the Damned played at the Roxy, supported by Eater. Spotted in the audience were Jimmy Page and Robert Plant from Led Zeppelin. 'I came down with Jimmy Page to check out the Damned,' said Plant. 'I was impressed by them, thought they were good, especially Rat Scabies, the drummer. He's really got it....All the talk about Old Farts and Young Farts is nonsense, age doesn't matter.'

company. The tune 'Carbona Not Glue', a song on their latest LP about sniffing the solvent Carbona, was causing a certain controversy. The UK record company MD demanded that the track be removed and replaced with a song called 'Babysitter'.

The New York school was busy giving birth. At the beginning of March Television, who had signed to Elektra, released their classic debut album "Marquee Moon", a punk landmark. It was swiftly followed by a European tour on which the group were rapturously received. (When their second album failed to receive a similar reception the next year, Verlaine broke up the group.)

But there was no reason for Tom Verlaine's group to feel secure in its position as then current kings of the Big Apple's rock'n'roll avant garde. A few days later, for example, Talking Heads had their first single out, 'Love a Building on Fire/New Feeling'. The group was made up of guitarist David Byrne, drummer Chris Frantz, bassist Tina Weymouth and its most recent recruit, keyboards player Jerry Harrison.

Exceptionally non-pc, the extremely angry Stranglers seemed almost a genre to themselves.
Bottom left: (left to right) Jet Black (drums), Hugh Cornwall (vocals, guitars),
Dave Greenfield (keyboards), Jean-Jaques Burnel (bass)

The Stranglers were no strangers to controversy: criticised for the sexism of their hit 'Peaches', the group ensured that at their next live show, an open-air event in Battersea Park, the audience were treated to a performance by a pair of strippers.

The notion of the Clash as militant, 'political' punk group, a favourite media projection, was not especially accurate. 'Like trousers, like brain,' Strummer's famous edict in The Battle Against Flared Trousers was at most an oblique artistic statement.

Certainly all the group were to the left of the political spectrum, but there was no alliance to any particular hardline doctrine. Instead, in the manner of reggae tunes, the songs of the Clash operated like telegrams to the masses, chronicling the events and attitudes of Britain that weren't considered newsworthy in the straight media. If the Clash dealt with any specific politics at all, they were the politics of the human condition. As Paul Simonon explained to a fan, on the night in July 1978 that he and Joe were arrested in Glasgow outside the Glasgow Apollo, 'It's not politics. It's just the difference between right and wrong.'

One shouldn't overlook, however, the element of the situationist scam that the group's manager, the ceaselessly obtuse Bernie Rhodes, introduced from his alliance with Malcolm McLaren. 'CBS couldn't understand the way I work. See, I like the idea of performance art, of seeing how far you can push something. It's like blowing up a photograph and finding out how long people see it as an image before they start seeing it as dots.' It should not be forgotten that early in their career Rhodes gave the Clash a pile of copies of *International Times*, borrowed from *NME* photographer Joe Stevens, with the suggestion that they find subject-matter for their songs in some of the underground paper's stories.

The 'political' tag also suggested a bunch of po-faced, finger-wagging preachers. It took little account of the absurdist humour that could make you laugh out loud whilst listening to Joe Strummer's lyrics. 'I think some of it's really hysterical stuff,' Joe agreed. 'We all used to burst out laughing too, when we first started playing them.' Strummer's speciality was a kind of punk version of Shakespearian asides: see, for example, how the phrase 'vacuum-cleaner sucks up budgie' - a headline from a copy of the *News of the World* newspaper that was lying around the studio - in 'Magnificent 7' becomes one of the funniest rock'n'roll lines ever. See also: 'Run, rabbit, run' in 'Bankrobber'; and the cry of 'Johnny, Johnny' in the condom saga 'Protex Blue'. In fact, all the Clash were very funny people.

Being part of the foundations of punk's self-help philosophy bathed all four members with an aura of warm positivity that could hardly fail to touch anyone who saw them. And it set the Clash up in sharp contrast to the abrasive nihilism of the Sex Pistols. But whatever the specifics of the politics, it all seemed incredibly important at the time, as though everyone concerned was taking part in a real revolution. Which, in fact, they probably were.

From the beginning the Sex Pistols and the Clash were rivals; they seemed to be played off against each other in the same way as the Rolling Stones and the Beatles profitably had been. The two managers genuinely were rivals. This was as a consequence of Rhodes having been rejected by McLaren in his efforts to form a united punk front – which would of course have compromised McLaren financially. Rhodes even tried to get CBS to give him a punk label on which the Pistols could also release records, only abandoning his attempts when McLaren made clear his lack of interest.

Despite all their contradictions the Clash were surrounded by stark poetry and synchronicities, a clear example of flowing with the force: if, as Mick Jones suspected, anyone was out to get the Clash, it was Babylon itself, whose existence the group sometimes seemed directly set up to counter. The group seemed, in Robert Raschenberg's phrase, 'to live in the gap between art and life'. This was partially down to their own artistic backgrounds – and also because of what had drawn them to those artistic backgrounds.

The Clash were steeped in that same British art-school tradition that had provided the creative launch-pad for many seminal UK rock'n'roll artists of the previous decade: John Lennon, Keith Richards, Pete Townshend, and Ray Davies. Whilst Mick Jones had been to art school in Shepherd's Bush, Paul Simonon had studied art at the Byam Shaw college in nearby Holland Park; Joe Strummer, meanwhile, had spent a year at London's Central School of Art before quitting his course. 'Rock'n'roll really is an art form – the most immediate there is, the most vital in terms of reaching out to the masses,' Mick Jones believed.

In the end, the Clash became a great piece of art, a panoramic living movie of a multiplicity of themes, incorporating all manner of contradictions and clarity.

It was the rhythm of reggae – whether you could hear it in specific songs or not – that was the heartbeat of the Clash. Reggae was certainly the coolest music to be into in 1975 and 1976 – largely because it seemed the only form that was progressing in any way – and it was just one more of the right credentials for the Clash.

The Clash were the first group to integrate Jamaican sounds fully into their music. By the time they played Bond's in Manhattan in 1981, which kicked the group up to an almost legendary level in the USA, much of the set seemed to consist of sprawling dub, as though you were listening to a sound system in one of London's Jamaican shebeens.

Joe Strummer had been into reggae for a long time, ever since Mole from the 101'ers had turned him onto it by nonstop playing of Big Youth's 'Screaming Target' LP. When the Clash recorded Junior Murvin's 'Police And Thieves' he was at first nervous of seeming 'naff', the 1977 equivalent of white-men-play-the-blues. How could Joe possibly emulate Junior Murvin's 'feathery voice'? he wondered. Yet 'Police and Thieves' became the standard bearer for the reggae/punk crossover that was chronicled in Bob Marley's 'Punky Reggae Party', produced by Lee "Scratch" Perry, who'd produced the Murvin record, as well as The Clash's 'Complete Control'. 'We were looking for a reggae production, but he wanted to learn how to do a punk production,' said Joe.

Mick Jones on the rivalry Malcolm McLaren fostered between the Sex Pistols and the Clash : 'There was this time when that feeling of being second-best was really getting to us. And, of course, Malcolm would help it along by throwing in some story like, oh Christ, there was this time when we heard that the Pistols had come over and nicked some of our gear. As a gesture of contempt, so to speak.

'So we'd immediately be up in arms...like, y'know, "let's get 'em, let's go over to their rehearsal place and rip off their microphones," always something petty. Like there was this time – the first time – the Pistols actually slagged us off in print, in a Melody Maker interview, I think it was – so, right we got off together and confronted John (Rotten) in a pub and John was pretty shocked, probably because he saw how petty we were all becoming, fighting among ourselves, just stupid squabbling when there was a very real enemy out there probably laughing its head off.'

6

In punk's eye of the hurricane, the Sex Pistols, things were taking their by now characteristic chaotic course. John Lydon and Glen Matlock loathed each other, Lydon despising the group's bass-player even more than he did the other group members. The most conventionally musical member of the group, Matlock was also a genuine, straightforward individual. John Lydon also thought of himself as genuine and straightforward but his artistic development unquestionably had been at the expense of the rest of his personality. As is the case with many artists, it was Lydon's deep self-justifying dysfunctionalism that was the source of his work. Increasingly, he and Malcolm McLaren were similar animals, manipulative, wilful, awful – there were close parallels in their speaking voices, those of petulant, whining, camp, slightly theatrical know-it-alls. Neither was capable of taking on board the opinions of anyone else. All the same, for whatever reason it was John 'Johnny Rotten' Lydon's task to be an archetype for disaffected youth. And the loathing and resentment projected onto him by Establishment thinking was an immensely heavy load to bear.

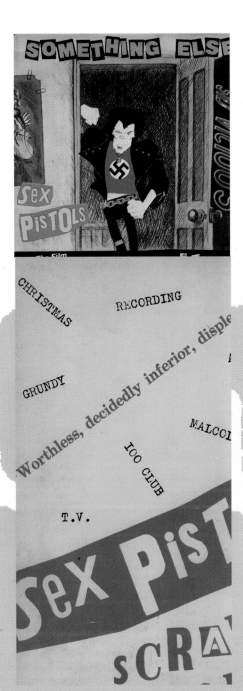

On 11 February Rotten's close friend Sid Vicious was tried out as a potential Sex Pistols' bass-player. Two days later, in a telephone interview with LA radio's adoring Anglophile Rodney Bingenheimer, Sid informed his interrogator that he was now a member of the group. No-one, however, seemed to have bothered to tell this to Glen Matlock. Matlock, in his turn, had almost had enough of playing with the Pistols – the writer of most of their songs' melodies, he was not at all happy with Lydon's controversial lyrics and was feeling increasingly disillusioned with continuing to play with him.

On Monday, 28 February Malcolm McLaren sent telegrams to the London music press, reporting that Glen Matlock had been ousted. Matlock, however, insisted that he had left of his own volition, and announced his intention to form a group called the Rich Kids.

On 10 March 1977 the career of the Sex Pistols as media *bêtes noires* hit another gear. That day they signed to A&M Records, on a table quickly set up on the pavement outside Buckingham Palace. After photographers had been briefly satisfied and the group had jumped back into their limousine before the police could intervene, they headed for a press conference at the Regent Palace Hotel on the edge of Soho. Malcolm McLaren dominated the event, announcing that the first single from the Pistols on A&M would be 'God Save the Queen'. Playing the Pistols-banned-from-playing card that he manipulated so adroitly, he threatened that if the group continued not to be allowed to play in Britain, then they might well leave the country for somewhere they were allowed to play.

The Sex Pistols then went back to A&M's New King's Road offices and created mayhem, Steve Jones goosing secretaries and Sid smashing a toilet bowl.

That Saturday night the Sex Pistols and their entourage went down to the Speakeasy, a rock'n'roll bar and club situated behind London's Oxford Circus. Also present in the club was disc jockey Bob Harris. The *Old Grey Whistle Test* TV music show that he presented was a paean to progressive rock – 'mock rock', 'Whispering' Bob had sniggered when the New York Dolls had appeared on the programme.

At the 'Speak' that night Harris was with a group called Bandit. When John 'Wobble' Wardle approached the DJ and asked why he didn't play the Pistols on his TV show, Harris's response was immediate and curt: 'We don't want the Sex Pistols on the programme. Does that answer your question?'

Not quite the right sort of reply. After Sid was then pushed by one of Bandit, he grabbed his glass and went for Harris, the rest of the Pistols right behind him. In the resulting scuffle a glass was broken over the head of Harris's friend, recording engineer George Nicholson. As a consequence Nicholson needed fourteen stitches to

Tony James with guitarist Derwood (proper).

The final line-up of Generation X, featuring (left to right) stalwarts Billy Idol, Tony James, James Stephenson, formerly of Chelsea, and Terry 'Tory Crimes' Chimes, the original Clash drummer. The 'proper' version of the group had Mark Laff on drums and Bob 'Derwood' Andrews on guitar.

hold together the wound.

On 16 March 1977, exactly a week after they had signed to the label, the Sex Pistols were dropped by A&M, a personal decision on the part of managing director Derek Green. All copies of 'God Save the Queen', which had already been pressed up on the A&M label, were scrapped. A mood of depression and resignation came over the Pistols' camp. As ever trying to turn their denial to advantage, McLaren and the group attempted to blame the firing by Derek Green on the responses of artists like Rick Wakeman, the personification of the Boring Old Fart, to the group being signed to the label for which he also recorded. There was no truth in this whatsoever - although it is always convenient to have someone else to blame.

For the group who had been set up as the Pistols' arch-rivals, there was only forward progression, however.

On 11 March the Clash played at a venue called the Harlesden Roxy, a club more regularly associated with performances by touring Jamaican acts. The show was a trial run for the group's upcoming 'White Riot' tour; also on the bill were the Buzzcocks, Subway Sect, and the Slits. This was the last date that

Paul Simonon on the Clash's respectful view of Bernie Rhodes: 'I always really overdid things with Bernie. There was one time we were all waiting to go off to Paris to play a concert. Bernie's sitting there in the garden in his deck-chair, reading the Sunday papers in the sun. And I'm pissing about in his house whilst Mick and Joe are moaning and wandering about. So I went out and got this hose and they both said, "No, don't do that!" But I turned the hose on Bernie and sprayed him all over. And he hates getting his hair wet - if it rains he runs down the road with his leather jacket over his head. So he just ran off, leaving the Sunday papers all crumpled up in the mud.'

Terry Chimes would play with the Clash at this time: although libelled on their first album cover by being given the name 'Tory Crimes', Chimes was too much of his own man to be prepared to harness his beliefs and ability in the way that he was being required to.

The next week the Clash released 'White Riot', their first single, inspired by the Notting Hill Carnival riot the previous year in which Joe Strummer, Paul Simonon and Bernie Rhodes had been caught up. 'It ain't punk, it ain't new wave, it's the next logical progression for groups to move in. Call it what you want - all the terms stink. Just call it rock and roll,' Mick Jones told the *NME*. The single made number 38 in the UK charts.

Meanwhile, in other news, Bob Andrews of Generation X was hit on the head by a can of beer at Leicester University. He was discharged from hospital after treatment. The hail of gob and other missiles that would greet punk acts as they toured Britain was almost beyond belief. What on earth was going on? What on earth had been unleashed? Punk groups stepping out on stage played the part of public whipping-post, as the audience's rage, envy and hate was physically projected onto them.

Later that month, on 25 March, Elvis Costello released his debut record, 'Less Than Zero', coupled with 'Radio Sweetheart', on Stiff Records (motto: *If it ain't Stiff, it ain't worth a fuck*). Reviewing the single in the *NME*, Charles Shaar Murray remarked: 'Great record. Doesn't have a snowball's chance in hell. What a bleedin' shame.'

A few days later Stiff released its first compilation, 'A Bunch Of Stiffs', comprised of its first ten singles, all of which had now been deleted: the LP included songs from Nick Lowe, Wreckless Eric, Elvis Costello, Motorhead, Magic Michael, Graham Parker, and the Tyla Gang.

In the light of the success of their main rivals the Clash, the Sex Pistols seemed in danger of seriously floundering. On 28 March they played a show at Notre Dame Hall, attached to the Notre Dame Catholic church in Leicester Place in the centre of London - this was to become a familiar venue for punk 'secret' gigs, and the Clash, who specialised in such 'events', were also to play there.

On 3 April the Pistols played The Screen on the Green cinema once again, with The Slits opening for them.

Two days later, however, Malcolm McLaren was informed by CBS Records that they had no interest in signing the group. Richard Branson, the owner of resolutely hippie label Virgin, was expressing enthusiasm, however. Meanwhile, Sid was hospitalised after developing hepatitis from the heroin habit at which he was working so hard.

And after all this time with two supposed record deals, all the Pistols had had out so far had been one single. Now on 7 April the Clash had their own eponymously titled first album released. Buyers of the album who'd found a red sticker in their LP were able to send in to the *NME* for an additional Clash record. This was made up of a performance of 'Capital Radio' - Joe had been fined for spray-painting the group's name on the walls of the London station - and an interview with the *NME*'s Tony Parsons. 'When I saw the Pistols,' Joe said in it, 'I suddenly realised that I wasn't alone in the fact that I couldn't play too well. I was in a group where all the people could play quite well and I felt inferior, and when I saw the Pistols I thought it was great. It just suddenly struck me that it didn't have to matter that much.'

In the inner sanctum of punk there were no more than about one hundred people: the Pistols and their hangers-on, the Clash and their hangers-on, the Bromley contingent, the various spin-offs from London SS, including the Damned, Generation X and Chrissie Hynde. It was a cliquey, non-supportive world: despite punk's many claims for being a people's music, a 'street' phenomenon, those at the core of punk would look down on the movement's dog soldiers, with their bin-liners and their safety-pins through their cheeks.

Notwithstanding the elitist, snotty moans, however, it was abundantly clear that something else - beyond outlaws, beyond outsiders - was taking over. By the warm spring of 1977 armies of multi-zippered, self-mutilating mutants were parading about London, like bit-players in a J G Ballard urban reality fantasy. It was a harsh statement, all that black leather and black hair, one from which the fashion world has yet to recover to this day. Rock'n'roll had exploded upon a deathly grey world twenty years previously; ten years before the peacocks of 'Swinging London' had been in power; now flared, wide-tied London suddenly had a difficult subplot, an awkward counterpoint, an army of hundreds and thousands of black-clad, spiky hairs, ready for wot-ever. *No Future!!!!!*

Punk's lumpen proles were now being snatched up by record companies. In the middle of April the Vibrators signed to CBS, to the irritation of the Clash. A few days later the Stranglers released 'IV Rattus Norvegicus', an album comprised entirely of original material that sold extremely well - despite, or because of, its violent and sexist themes.

By the end of the month the Adverts had released their first single, 'One Chord Wonders', on Stiff. The Jam, meanwhile, released *their* first single, 'In The City', on 29 April . Although not part of punk's inner sanctum, which ultimately may have led to audiences identifying with them as underdogs, the Jam had a snowballing popularity, and the high energy single, which displayed leader Paul Weller's Rickenbacker guitar, sold well.

Stymied by the departure of Terry Chimes, the Clash had been feverishly auditioning new drummers. In Paris on 27 April for Nuits de Punk, the group brought a new drummer with them called Nicky 'Topper' Headon, who they were 'trying out'. With Topper in the driving-seat, the group played at Eric's, a new music club, in Liverpool on 5 May . At the show one Pete Wylie met a certain Julian Cope, who was dancing in front of him; Wylie introduced Cope to another friend of his, Ian McCulloch. Later, they would all have their own successful groups: Wylie's Wah Heat!, Cope's Teardrop Explodes, McCulloch's Echo And The Bunnymen.

Most of May was taken up with the 'White Riot' tour, another version of the same kind of punk package that the Pistols had attempted the previous December. The Jam, the Buzzcocks, Subway Sect, and the Slits were the other acts on the bill.

None of the shows was banned this time, as they trekked around the country, with a busload of friends and hangers-on, including Chrissie Hynde. Staying in reasonably expensive hotels, the Clash would double up the various support acts, letting them sleep on their floors or spare beds. It was complete chaos, and it seemed hardly surprising when the police stopped the group's bus on 21 May after their St Albans gig and found some pillows from the Newcastle Holiday Inn: Strummer and Topper Headon were charged with theft.

On 9 May the tour had played the Rainbow in Finsbury Park. It was to be the last show from the Jam, who quit the package to headline their own shows - their first album had been released on 6 May. Although Bernie Rhodes had endeavoured to persuade the venue's management to remove the seating from the front stalls, he had been unsuccessful. Throughout the Clash's performance, therefore, pogoing fans smashed the seats to matchwood, pieces of them being passed up onto the front of the stage where the pile gradually grew larger and larger. Such a punk demolition of one of rock's most sacred temples seemed more like a confirmed takeover than some attempt at mild insurrection. It was considered a major victory, and for onlookers proved hilariously funny.

It was hardly surprising, however, that in the end the Clash - who had to pay for the smashed Rainbow seats, all 200 of them - lost £28,000 on the tour.

The Clash were also finding that they were to pay the cost of signing with CBS. On 13 May , without consulting the group, the company had taken 'Remote Control' off their album and put it out as a single. It was to be the first of a seemingly endless series of rows between the group and the record company; 'Complete Control', one of the group's finest records, produced by Lee 'Scratch' Perry, was released later in the year, on 23 September , like an answer record to the company: *They said, we'll make loads of money/And worry about it later.*

On 12 May Virgin Records had announced that they had signed the Pistols. By now the hepatitis-stricken Sid had been released from hospital, where Nancy Spungen has been his most regular visitor. With 'God Save the Queen' already recorded and waiting in the wings to go, it was rush-released, in the shops a week later. The Pistols were turned down by Thames TV for a ten-second ad spot during *Today*.

The single 'God Save the Queen' had been released so quickly in order not to miss Jubilee week at the beginning of the next month.

Richard Branson, multi-millionaire airline magnate and pensions guru, dabbles in punk rock.

The Slits were extraordinary. Creating the template for the coming deluge of female groups, their world was the infinite space suggested by dub. Formed in January 1977 they consisted of guitarist Viv Albertine, drummer Palm Olive, bass-player Tessa Pollitt, and a fourteen-year old singer called Ari Upp. Their first album 'Cut', produced by Dennis Bovell was a landmark LP.

Yes FUTURE !

GABBA GABBA HEY

7

The Ramones' exhortation 'Gabba Gabba Hey!' – onstage Joey Ramone would brandish a black and yellow banner bearing this arcane message – came from its use in the chorus of their song 'Pinhead'. In turn this originated from Tod Browning's 1932 oddity film *Freaks*, set in a travelling circus: during a wedding ceremony between a midget and a woman, the assembled throng begin chanting 'Gobble gobble, we accept her, one of us'. When the Ramones were recording 'Pinhead', for the album "The Ramones Leave Home", they had intended to use this same chant, but, for added power, permitted it to mutate.

Even the sun shone for it: the punk rock summers of 1976 and 1977 were the hottest weather in the UK for over thirty years, in those days before heat from another planet could induce fear. In early September 1976, as the Thames had visibly receded to a fat stream and the mud-banks at its side dried up and cracked, it had seemed like a vision of a science-fiction future was being enacted in London's streets.

Everything seemed italicised by the relentless glare from the monoxide red ball in the sky. Those who searched out meanings in signs and portents considered the unseasonably hot weather to be not without significance. How life had suddenly speeded up only became apparent later.

Whatever, the way that so much of the country's official energies already seemed to be girded to fighting the evil of punk rock was extraordinary. It certainly felt as though a revolution of some sort was taking place, a revolution of the spirit, which it almost certainly was. You could sense it those summers, all around you. It was very uplifting and very funny, and sometimes extremely sinister.

The sheer pointlessness and arrogance of the Jubilee celebrations was the catalyst that brought it all to a head. The nation now seemed torn in two.

By Jubilee weekend 'God Save the Queen' had already sold 150,000 copies. Malcolm McLaren and Virgin owner Richard Branson sought another promotional stunt. On Monday, 7 June, a holiday to permit the nation to celebrate the glories of the Jubilee, a boat-trip along the Thames was planned, a satirical precursor to the Queen's own scheduled river procession through London on 9 June.

At 6.15 in the evening 175 people, including the Sex Pistols, met at Charing Cross Pier in the centre of London to board a riverboat named – naturally – the *Queen Elizabeth*.

THE RAMONES

The Ramones are not an oldies group, they are not a glitter group, they don't play boogie music and they don't play the blues. The Ramones are an original Rock and Roll group of 1975, and their songs are brief, to the point and every one a potential hit single.

The quartette consists of Johnny, Joey, Dee Dee and Tommy Ramone. Johnny, the guitarist, plays with such force that his sound has been compared to a hundred howitzers going off. Joey, the lead singer, is an arch villain whose lanky frame stands threatening center stage. Dee Dee is Bass guitar and the acknowledged handsome one of the group, and Tommy is the drummer whose pulsating playing launches the throbbing sound of the band.

The Ramones all originate from Forest Hills and kids who grew up there either became musicians, degenerates or dentists. The Ramones are a little of each. Their sound is not unlike a fast drill on a rear molar.

Contact Tome Erdelyi
Loudmouth Productions
65-35 Yellowstone Blvd.
Forest Hills, N. Y. 11375
777-0231
263-8908

Tommy Ramone on the Ramones: 'It was a new way of looking at music. We took the rock sound into a psychotic world and narrowed it down into a straight line of energy...We used block chording as a melodic device, and the harmonics resulting from the distortion of the amplifiers created countermelodies.'

Tony James: 'The Ramones were the single most important group that changed punk rock. When their album came out, all the English groups tripled speed overnight. Two-minute-long songs, very fast. The Pistols were almost the only group who stuck to the kind of Who speed. People forget that punk rock was both incredibly intelligent and very funny.'

Jerry Nolan: 'When Johnny and I got to England, everybody became junkies, almost overnight.'

The boat ploughed its course up and down the river. After about three hours the group set up and launched into 'Anarchy in the UK', followed by 'God Save the Queen', and then an abbreviated set - 'No Feelings', 'Pretty Vacant', 'I Wanna Be Me', 'No Fun'.

The *Queen Elizabeth*, however, was being shadowed by six police boats, which ordered the captain to pull over to the nearest pier, Charing Cross.

As the boat's passengers eventually disembarked, they ran foul of the irritable representatives of law and order: eleven people were arrested, including Vivienne Westwood and Malcolm McLaren who tactfully called the police 'fucking fascist bastards', as the Pistols were smuggled off the boat by a side exit.

In the world that existed aside from the two main contenders, the Sex Pistols and the Clash, there was a flurry of creative activity. As 1977 had progressed, so had the speed of record releases and group formations: the number of classic singles released during the course of the year was extraordinary. In the middle of May, for example, Nick Lowe released an EP - 'Bowi, Pure Pop for Now People', a slightly twee parody of the last Bowie album, entitled 'Low'; also on Stiff, Elvis Costello's second single was released - 'Alison', coupled with 'Welcome to the Working Week'; in time for their UK tour the Ramones had a new single released, 'Sheena is a Punk Rocker'; on 20 May the Heartbreakers had their first single out, 'Chinese Rocks', the title of which amply described an influence that Johnny Thunders was indiscriminately spreading around him on the punk scene.

Miles Copeland, the brother of Stewart, drummer with the Police had formed his own label, Step Forward, something he undoubtedly was attempting to do. Copeland had signed both Bristol group the Cortinas and Chelsea. From Chelsea he put out 'Right To Work', a song sneered at by the punk elite - who, despite the unemployment figures, considered punk to be about the right *not* to work - but considered by those more distant, like the American rock critic Dave Marsh, to be a classic of the genre.

At the end of the month a group called the Stiff Kittens opened the show at Manchester's Electric Circus, supporting the Buzzcocks, Penetration and John Cooper Clarke. Soon the group changed their name to Warsaw, before settling on Joy Division.

Talking Heads, meanwhile, were drawing accolades on their first UK tour, supported by Blondie and Squeeze, another act managed by Miles Copeland. In Belfast an up-and-coming punk act went by the name of Stiff Little Fingers. In a neat, ironic twist, meanwhile, the Rich Kids had found their fourth member in Midge Ure, who had once been asked to join the Pistols as singer.

The Jam, moreover, announced that they would imminently drop the Union Jack imagery with which they had dabbled, a pastiche of pop art in the Mod manner. Their waving of the British flag had been misread as evidence of the trio's support for the extreme right. For a long time the Jam were subjected to doubts over their punk credentials - *after all, they came from Surrey* - and Joe Strummer even criticised them in his masterwork '(White Man) In Hammersmith Palais'; identifying the Jam by their 'Burton suits', he dismissed them as a new group 'not concerned with what there is to be learned'.

In a way the Jubilee was the zenith of punk. Even though the music business conspired to keep them off the top of the charts, everyone knew the Sex Pistols really had been number one during Jubilee Week - desperate no doubt for later knighthoods, the BMRB (British Market Research Bureau), from whom *Top Of The Pops* took their charts, may have pretended they were at number two, to Rod Stewart's 'I Don't Want To Talk About It', but in the Virgin shops the Pistols were outselling Rod by two to one. Certainly they were at number one in the *NME. What a stunt to pull off!* It was very, very funny. But it seemed to bring all the crazies out too, on whatever side they could be found.

Rotten on being attacked in the pub carpark: 'They were...uhh...loyal to their Queen. That's why they jumped me. "We like our Queen. How dare you?"..While I was being pounded to pieces I was just thinking "Ell. Oh, this is just so absurd." You have to laugh because it is so...Where do they come from??? It's hardly a nice way of them displaying their liking for their Queen, is it now? Anyway, that record was good. I liked it. Brought a lot of people out of their closets. Everyone hated her before but nobody said it.'

John Cooper Clarke: Make mine Majorca...

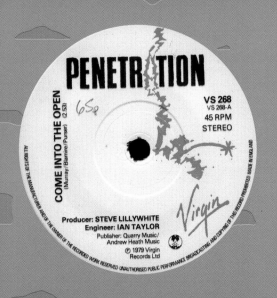

PENETRATION
COME INTO THE OPEN
(2:53)
(Murray/Blamire/Purser)
VS 268
VS 268-A
45 RPM
STEREO

Producer: STEVE LILLYWHITE
Engineer: IAN TAYLOR
Publisher: Quarry Music/
Andrew Heath Music
℗ 1979 Virgin
Records Ltd

Virgin

Left: *Gang of Four -
rigour was their middle name.*

Below: *Rezillos - extremely Scottish.*

Top left: *Glen Matlock's Rich Kids -
Ghosts of Princes in Towers.*
Bottom left: *Modettes -
what had the Slits started?*

THE .DEFECTS
1. GUILTY CONSCIENCE
2. BRUTALITY

45 rpm   side 2   CR001

**CASUALTY
RECORDS**

86

Feargal Sharkey of Londonderry's Undertones, briefly the New Beatles.

Tony James: 'Mods and rockers fought each other. Punk rock fought the Establishment. It pointed a finger at the monarchy, a very touchy subject – it wasn't a soap opera then.'

On 18 June John Rotten, as he was now known by his friends, and record producer Chris Thomas were attacked in the car park of a north London pub close to Wessex studios where the Pistols were recording. Slashed by a razor as he was attempting to get away in Thomas's car, he required two stitches in his arm, a tendon being badly damaged.

The next evening at Shepherd's Bush tube station inoffensive Paul Cook was given such a beating by five men carrying knives and a metal bar that he needed fifteen stitches in the back of his head. Was the aggression and violence courted by the Pistols in the early days of the group rebounding on them? The previous week Jamie Reid, who designed the Pistols' artwork, had been attacked near his south London flat, receiving a broken leg and nose.

On 1 July, with 'God Save the Queen' still high in the charts, Virgin rush-released another single, 'Pretty Vacant'. Ostensibly a safe pop song, the only hint of subversion came in the chorus line: *We're so pretty, oh so pretty, vay-cunt.* The record was put out behind the back of Malcolm McLaren, who was in Los Angeles attempting to secure the group a movie deal; this film was to become McLaren's obsession for the remaining life of the Pistols.

Now, to promote the single, the Pistols even appeared on *Top of the Pops*, the high-audience weekly BBC chart show: Virgin made a promotional film of the group performing 'Pretty Vacant', which was screened on the programme.

To McLaren's fury, John Lydon also appeared in an extensive radio interview on London's Capital Radio, being interviewed by DJ Tommy Vance as he played his favourite records. After the interview, Lydon was perceived to be a man of considerable intelligence, an impression greatly at odds with the image his manager had attempted to foster. Malcolm McLaren was enraged, especially about a series of remarks his charge made about him on the show: 'It's fashionable to believe that Malcolm McLaren dictates to us but that's just not true. What really amuses me about Malcolm is the way they say he controls the press: media manipulator. The point of it all is that he did nothing: he just sat back and let them garble out their own rubbish.'

The Sex Pistols then left the country, for two weeks of Scandinavian dates.

Andy Czezowski's tenure at the Roxy had ended on 30 April: the club's owners decided they could run a similar policy themselves.

Rotten : 'Nobody's ever come that close to doing what we did...being either really liked or really hated – but no-one ignored it. What a joke. And the other members – Steve and Paul – were not even aware of it. Not even vaguely. Didn't want to know. Always struck me as funny, that.'

Did John Rotten consider himself A Punk? 'No! I refute that term. It was ridiculous. I hate that name. I think it's loathsome. And I particularly hated the people who took it upon themselves to go around calling themselves punks. They didn't have the mentality to suss out that that was pure media walking all over them. People always get it wrong.'

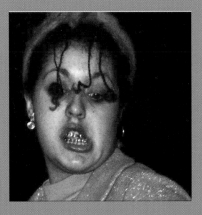

Poly Styrene: 'The weird thing about all the plastic is that people don't actually like it, but in order to cope with it they develop a perverse kind of fondness for it, which is what I did.'

Poly Styrene: 'Young kids would come around dressed up from Seditionaries and they're probing me about all these rumours that they've heard about me. Such sexual questions; they must be perverts, you know what I mean? If you can't sort sex out for yourself there must be something a bit wrong with you....I think a lot of kids are hung up about sex and that's bad.'

The Acme accountant tried to open another club, at a discotheque in Wardour Street called Crackers. Again, he was stitched up, and the club's owners took the mantle of providing punk on Monday and Tuesday nights onto themselves. Accordingly, on 4 July Crackers transmogrified into the Vortex, with performances that night from a trio of Manchester acts: the Buzzcocks, new act the Fall, and poet-comedian John Cooper Clarke. Vile bouncers hovered menacingly.

The next day director Derek Jarman began shooting *Jubilee*, a 'punk film' starring Jenny Runacre, Richard O'Brien, Little Nell, Jordan, and Adam and the Ants. Sneered at by the punk elite, the film turned out to be a clever encapsulation of the state of Britain in the summer of 1977.

At the end of the month the Jam topped the bill in their first major London concert, at the Hammersmith Odeon. Generation X, meanwhile, signed to Chrysalis, and had queues down Wardour Street when they played the Marquee. The Adverts had signed to Anchor, and their 'Gary Gilmore's Eyes' single was set for late August. The Stranglers had another hit, not off their album, 'Something Better Change'. In the world of Miles Copeland, who was fast emerging as a punk entrepreneur, Squeeze released their first record, 'A Packet of Three'. And the Police played their last dates as a four-piece, with the addition of guitarist Andy Summers.

On 26 July Elvis Costello played on the pavement of London's Park Lane, outside the Hilton hotel inside which the CBS convention was taking place: Costello's album "My Aim is True" had just been released, about to become a UK chart hit. As he and his manager Jake Riviera no doubt desired, Costello was arrested, with subsequent desirable publicity. Soon a deal would be struck in the USA with CBS. By now the irascible west London singer had quit his day job as a computer programmer at the Elizabeth Arden cosmetics factory.

Sid Vicious had to interrupt the Scandinavian tour to appear in court, on 2 August , charged with carrying a knife at the previous September's 100 Club Punk Festival. He was fined £125.

On 19 August, the Pistols played the Lafayette Club in Wolverhampton as the Spots (Sex Pistols On Tour). It was the first of several British dates: on 24 August, the group played as the Tax Exiles at the Outlook Club in Doncaster. Later in the week they peformed in Scarborough as Special Guest, in Middlesbrough as Acne Rabble, and in Plymouth as the Hamsters. McLaren announced that the group were having talks with Russ Meyer, soft-porn director of the cult classic *Beyond the Valley of the Dolls* and that a script was being written. As though this information was a mere footnote, McLaren also revealed that the group was readying their first album for release.

On the night of 11 August, Elvis Presley died – just over a month

The Members: Offshore Banking Business? (still unsure).

Rotten on the Tommy Vance Show, questioned about Punk Rock: 'A lot of it is real rubbish, I mean real rubbish, pathetic, and just giving it a bad name. A lot of bands are ruining it. They're either getting too much into the star trip or they're going the exact opposite way. Neither way is really honest. If you know what you're really doing you can completely ignore the whole damn thing which is what we've always done...'

On the programme, entitled *A Punk and His Music*, John Rotten played Bowie's 'Rebel Rebel', Tim Buckley's 'Sweet Surrender', Gary Glitter's 'All Right With The Boys', Captain Beefheart's 'It's the Blimp', Neil Young's 'Revolution Blues', Lou Reed's 'Men Of Good Fortune' – 'I don't like the Velvet Underground,' he pronounced, though he also featured songs by John Cale and Nico. And records by the Chieftains, Kevin Coyne, Peter Hammill, and his beloved Can. And there were some top ranking reggae tunes: Augustus Pablo's 'King Tubby Meets the Rockers Uptown', Culture's 'I'm Not Ashamed', Aswad's 'Jah Wonderful', and songs by Ken Boothe, the Gladiators, and Fred Locks. After he played Dr Alimantado's 'Born for a Purpose', Rotten described how that had been the record he came home and played following the beating he received with Chris Thomas.

'What would you like to say to people who like you?' questioned Vance.

'Big deal,' retorted Rotten.

The radio interview led to the *Sunday Times* describing Rotten as a 'mild-mannered liberal chap with a streets-of-Islington accent.'

Rotten on McLaren's fury over the Tommy Vance show: 'That was pathetic. It seemed to mean that if I liked records like that then I couldn't be half as ignorant, moronic, violent, destructive et cetera et cetera as they wanted to promote me as...But Malcolm's like that. He sees something in someone and thinks, "Oh, if only, if only..."Believes his own fuckin' lies.'

Rotten: 'They wanted me as some kind of cardboard cut-out they could wheel out and put on display.'

The Clash in Belfast -
they never got to play.

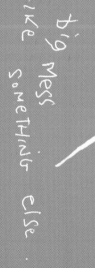

C-R-A-C-KKKKKKK.........
A police nightstick smashes down on the head of Paul Simonon. Standing aghast in the balmy carbon monoxide summer breeze of late-night Glasgow, the Clash bass-player crumples to his knees, and then to the ground. The burly plain-clothes detective who – for no reason whatosever – has tried literally to bring Simonon down to earth pulls his arms behind his back and handcuffs him, wrenching him to his feet.

In the distance Joe Strummer, his hands secured behind his back, is being shoved into a police van. His crime? To have thrown a plastic bottle of lemonade to the ground outside the stage-door of the Glasgow Apollo – his despairing, anguished response to a thirteen-year-old girl fan telling him how the venue's bouncers had taken punk fans down an alley and beaten them up, a response to Strummer's fevered demand that the 'kids' be allowed to dance to the Clash's show. During their performance of '(White Man) In Hammersmith Palais', open warfare seems to break out between the group and the venue's 'security'. Now it looks as though the bouncers have set them up with their friends in the local police force. Mick Jones stands in tears as he witnesses this legal debacle.

Thrown into the same cell together, Strummer and Simonon make full use of the bass-player's multi-zippered pants, snorting up the small packet of cocaine stashed in one of the secret compartments.

In court the next day Joe Strummer and Paul Simonon both plead guilty to 'causing a public nuisance'; they are given a small fine and discharged. There are sufficient witnesses: why haven't they pleaded not guilty?

'Taking on the British establishment's a mug's game,' Strummer defends himself, as the group's hire car purrs away to their next show, in Aberdeen. 'Let them think they've won. Then get on to the next town and spread the message. But if they don't want to come to the Promised Land, I ain't gonna take them by the hand and lead them there.'

90

Steve Jones turned up at several Clash shows during the Out On Parole tour. Mick Jones would find himself sharing the stage with the former Sex Pistol during encores. It was not until he thought to ask that Jones discovered precisely why the man who shared his surname kept appearing at these Clash dates: because Bernie Rhodes had told him he was due to replace Mick Jones in the Clash.

Not only did Bernie Rhodes attempt to move Steve Jones into the Clash to replace Mick Jones during the summer of 1978, but Malcolm McLaren had attempted to poach Paul Simonon to be Pistols' bass-player at the end of 1977 when Sid was plainly becoming completely out-of-control.

Joe Strummer: 'Bernie lost control of us. His scene was not to give us any money in case it ruined us, which is the way you deal with kids – which he thought we were. But he underestimated us. Like people say Bernie wrote our songs, but that's not true at all. All he said was, "Don't write love songs, write something that you care about, that's real." And it's a pity we fell out with him 'cos we made a good team.

'But he got really funny when the Clash all started to happen. We wouldn't see him from week to week. If he wanted to communicate he'd just send a minion – implying he was too busy elsewhere to deal with us.

'You know "Complete Control" which Mick wrote about the record company. In fact we got the phrase off Bernie one night in that pub in Wardour Street, The Ship. I remember him going – he'd obviously been talking to Malcolm and was trying to be the master puppeteer – going, "Look, I want complete control, I want complete control". And we were just laughing at him.'

For about a year, Sham 69 were one of Britain's biggest groups. Their substantial far right following, however, compelled singer Jimmy Pursey, a genuinely likeable 'bloke', to break up the group - on several occasions. He was frequently in tears as his stage was overrun by Doc Marten-clad neo-nazis.

Hersham boys, Hersham boys / laced-up boots and corduroys

Jimmy Pursey: (as reported in the *NME*, 16 June, 1979): 'How do you think the lads feel when they see all this 'Pistols 69' crap in the papers? Sham 69 are still together, right? Steve and Paul have asked me to join the Sex Pistols and tour and if Sham finishes it finishes, but we're still going.'

Johnny Rotten thinks this about Jimmy Pursey: 'I certainly don't have to perform at being working class. There's so much made of it - as if the more dumb you are the more glorious you become. That's why Pursey is so well liked - because he plays his role for everyone. It's so easy to manipulate, it fits into a nice little cliched bracket - no threat. It's once you break that apart you become a worry to them."

later he was to be followed to rock'n'roll heaven by Marc Bolan, killed in a car crash in west London. To some there appeared to be a connection between the deaths of these 'dinosaur old farts' – punk's catch-all term of abuse – and the sweeping cultural changes taking place.

As a counterpoint to punk, which many record company employees still deeply loathed or were terrified of, a more palatable new form of music had been contrived – powerpop. Slotted into this conveniently broad term were acts like Glen Matlock's Rich Kids – on 29 August they played a surprise date at the Vortex, with Mick Jones guesting on guitar – and New Hearts, who signed to CBS. When unable to get out of discussions about punk, such record company types preferred the term 'New Wave', a term weighted with intellectual pretensions and lacking the sense of darkness now so often associated with 'punk'.

The next generation of punk groups was now emerging. On 12 August the Members played live at the under-old-management Roxy for the first time. The same month the Ruts – who were to become Virgin label-mates with the Members – were coming together in Southall, their initial intention being to form an occasional group as a pastime from their more regular work as a funk outfit. With their sub-Clash militant music – their first hit, in June 1979, was called 'Babylon's Burning' – they would have four top hits before Malcolm Owen, their lead singer, died of a heroin overdose the next July.

On 12 August, Sham 69 played the Roxy, to an ecstatic review from Tony Parsons in *NME*: 'Jimmy Pursey of Sham 69 is a star. Hardly anyone has heard of him or his band, he doesn't get interviewed by *Vogue* or *Sunday Times Magazine* and he probably don't pull any more birds than you do...Sham 69 are ex-skinheads who don't have the cash or the inclination to dazzle you with the mandatory sartorial elegance of corporate sponsored urban guerrillas. They're content to use their performance to provoke REACTION! God, I wish you could have been there. Sham 69 are a band who do everything except lie,' he concluded with all the characteristic hyperbolic hysteria of the young rock critic.

But the stories of officialdom trying to hold back the tide of youthful rebellion (which, Parsons was correct, was frequently underwritten by record company tour support) were unabated.

On 20 August Generation X encountered unexpected problems when they tried to play at Clouds in Edinburgh. The police turned up to inform the group that the club didn't have a music licence. Scrabbling around for somewhere to play, Generation X found a venue just outside Edinburgh at the last moment. 'We had to bus all the people to another place,' remembered Tony James. 'We didn't

It is August, 1977. In the bar of a hotel in the Belgian countryside sit the Clash, the Damned, and Elvis Costello and the Attractions: the room is a blur of coloured spiky hair, multi-zippered clothing, narrow-lapelled jackets, Slim Jim ties dangling loose. Accompanying Costello is his manager, Jake Riviera, the co-founder of Stiff Records and until very recently a stalwart of the now passé pub rock scene.

The three acts await their performances on that evening's 'Punk' bill at a three-day Belgian summer festival. But there are other styles of groups playing over the weekend. Look, one has just arrived. It is called Uriah Heep and these dinosaurs of cod underground rock are walking into the very same joint, and – in a big-haired, flared-trousered way – are stepping up to the bar.

They have not yet seen who are the sole occupants of this lowlands tavern. Before they do, Jake Riviera notices them. 'Ah, "Proud Words on a Dusty Shelf", eh Ken,' he calls out to Ken Hensley, Heep's 'creative' leader who recently has released a solo album with that title. '"Very 'Eavy, Very 'Umble",' Rat Scabies sneers the name of the first Uriah Heep album. 'Fuck off, old farts,' laughs Pete Thomas, the Attractions' drummer, launching a beer-mat in their direction.

In horror the four members of Uriah Heep turn and look at each other. As one they cross the bar and walk out through the door. Pop music will never be the same again.

That night Elvis Presley dies.

understand it at all. Generation X wasn't the most political of groups. When you're young it seems much more frightening. In the Sixties they put flowers in guns; in the Seventies we put pictures of guns and tanks on our record sleeves. It wasn't exactly meant to be a call to arms.'

All the stories of police suppression of punk seemed extraordinary, even at the time. One was slightly amazed that they really took it so seriously.

The next day, a Sunday night, Elvis Costello played at the Nashville. Over 1,000 people turned up, desperate to see the show. After the police were called eight arrests were made.

Coming just after a month after Costello had busked in Park Lane in front of the CBS convention, the confrontational thinking of Jake Riviera could be sensed in this latest shock horror outrage in which his artist found himself. In the wake of McLaren's ceaseless scamming, various other managers tried their hand at similar techniques. Riviera, who was later to claim to have moulded himself on controversial Led Zeppelin manager Peter Grant, had by far the most finesse of all these pretenders.

At Stiff Records, for example, he ensured that events continued to move apace. On 10 September Ian Dury, who had sung with Kilburn and the Highroads, had his first solo single released on Stiff - 'Sex & Drugs & Rock & Roll'. A witty anthem, the tune was an immensely important record, a trailer for Dury's "New Boots and Panties" album, released later in the month. Dury was now solidly established as the Godfather of Punk. On 28 September Stiff released "Stiff Greatest Stiffs", a compilation LP of the already deleted first ten singles on the label.

During September, in fact, there was a slew of further outstanding releases. The Clash put out their third single, 'Complete Control/City of the Dead'. X-Ray Spex - led by Poly Styrene who wore dental braces and whose real name was Marion Elliot - signed to Virgin and released 'Oh Bondage Up Yours'. With an impressive persona and lyrics, Poly became a sort of figurehead.

The Boomtown Rats had their first 45 out, 'Looking After Number One', which just missed making the Top Ten. And the Tom Robinson Band put out '2-4-6-8 Motorway', a sort of novelty record that got to number five. Meanwhile, the Stranglers released their second LP, 'No More Heroes', recorded at the same time as their first album - it was another substantial seller.

The punk atmosphere of violence, however, seemed now to be pan-European. In Sweden the Jam were pelted with chairs and had eggs thrown at them by the raggare, a group of rockers celebrated for causing trouble at punk and other gigs. Then the Jam's gear was trashed. They were forced to cancel a Dutch date as they no longer had enough gear with which to play.

Bob Geldof of the Boomtown Rats: 'I don't think I ever thrust myself on the press....When we got to England, it was really a long time before anyone really talked to us. And by the time people did start talking to us, I was so hungry to get something over to them that I had no hesitation to make a statement. I'd talked about things I believed in passionately, and the press mostly thought it was outrageous...And then when we had a hit, people thought "Where the fuck have these paddies come from?"' Geldof's finest hour by far was yet to come, in the summer of 1985, when he singlehandedly organised the LiveAid mercy concerts to help the starving of Ethiopia.

NEVER MIND

THE BO⬛⬛KS

Rotten: 'All that nonsense about us not being able to get gigs was just some weird managerial scheme. He thought he'd bury us in some kind of mystique and that would help record sales. He'd seen too many films, it was all his ridiculous, romantic image of himself. God, what a fiasco!'

Rotten on Pistols as political group: 'Name me one political move in any direction! The closest was "Anarchy" but that's not about politics, it's just about...music. As simple as that. I don't know where they got that political stance from. I know nothing about politics. It doesn't mean much who's in power anyway, does it? This country's so bland it could be Hitler and no-one would notice...except, of course, for the self-righteous SWP who I really loathe.
'......I just think it's ridiculous when they [SWP] and the NF get together and have their battle of the thugs. I don't think they realise that they're more self-righteous than Mary Whitehouse can ever hope to be.
'I don't like the NF, but I don't like the SWP either. I think they're both as evil as each other. Both a serious threat. God, can you imagine if this was a total Socialist country? How awful that would be: classical music being piped in the streets day and night, all wearing grey uniforms and cloth caps.'

Rotten: 'That's what ruined the Pistols - it was too much the opposite of what had gone before, thus it was too easily identifiable, too easy to understand and assimilate, no threat.'

On 23 September, the Vortex attempted to expand its territory, opening a twenty-four-hour coffee and record shop in Hanway Street, near Tottenham Court Road. At lunchtime Sham 69 arrived, set up on the roof and launched into a set: 'I Don't Wanna', 'George Davis is Innocent' and 'Ulster', before the police arrived to enact the inevitable arrest of vocalist Jimmy Pursey. The publicity thus engendered - they made that weekend's *Sunday Times* - clearly had nothing whatsoever to do with the fact that this happened to be the day of release of Sham's first EP, on Step Forward, produced by John Cale; the songs they performed were from the record: its sleeve used a picture of police dragging off a demonstrator at the Lewisham riot that had taken place on 23 August that year. By the end of the next month the group signed to Polydor.

But things were also falling apart. At the beginning of October, the Heartbreakers were touring Britain, promoting their 'LAMF' album, released in the late summer. It was not the only thing the group was promoting: the title of one song on the set, 'Chinese Rocks', amply described a further influence that Johnny Thunders was indiscriminately spreading around him on London's punk scene. His smack addiction was to be 'caught' by several other punk rock players.
Thunders' increasingly erratic, drug-induced behaviour, moreover, was having a negative effect on his own group. Even his long stalwart Jerry Nolan, himself no stranger to heroin addiction, was tiring of it. Midway through the tour Nolan suddenly announced that he was out of the group. After a phone-call from Johnny Thunders, Paul Cook turned up to dep on drums at a Saturday night date at Bristol Polytechnic, bringing with him Steve Jones to add further guitar parts. Both Pistols played with the Heartbreakers in a gig that carried all the now characteristic aggro of a punk night out: when soccer hooligans tried to trash the hall, they knocked the promoter unconscious. But at least Thunders' group got five encores. Soon Steve Jones was to join Sid Vicious as a heroin-addicted member of the Sex Pistols.
The next day, 2 October , Rat Scabies walked out on the Damned in the middle of a European tour, utterly disillusioned with the group's new LP, 'Music For Pleasure'; curiously, the album had been produced by Pink Floyd drummer Nick Mason. Temporarily replaced by Dave Berk from Johnny Moped, Rat told *Sounds*, 'The punk thing has become the quickest sell-out I've ever seen. Now it's completely run by businessmen. It's just a trend to make money out of. That was one of the main things getting me down. Instead of Boring Old Farts, we had Boring Young Farts. We were all getting fat, especially me and the Captain. Suddenly we were on £50 a week when we were used to a tenner on the dole. We had it easier than we'd ever had it in our life and with that the desperation went.'
And even the businessmen were falling out. On 3 October the Stiffs Greatest Stiffs Live Tour set off on the road, featuring Elvis Costello, Nick Lowe, Wreckless Eric, Larry Wallis and Ian Dury. Dury was backed by his new group, the Blockheads, with guitarist Chas Jankel, saxist Davey Payne, bassist Norman Watt-Roy and drummer Charley Charles.
But the next day Jake Riviera and Dave Robinson went their separate ways, Riviera leaving Stiff to Robinson and taking Elvis and Nick Lowe with him.

By contrast to the reality of their existence, one of terminal decline and ennui, the Pistols appeared to the outside world to be going through a phase of extraordinary productivity. By the end of the month the group had out their third single in six months, 'Holidays in the Sun', written in Berlin during a brief sojourn from being the British *bêtes noires*. The single's sleeve was ripped off from the artwork for a Belgian tourist brochure.
A satire on package holidays, the single was really a trailer for the group's album, clumsily titled 'Never Mind the Bollocks...Here's the Sex Pistols', and due for release on 4 November. There were advance orders in the UK of 125,000.

Nick Lowe, who in a low-key way was one of punk's most important figures.

Two weeks before the album's release, 'Spunk', a bootleg of an earlier mix, was already in certain shops. The hand of Virgin and McLaren was suspected of being behind this somewhat obvious piece of lateral marketing.

Out three days late on 7 November, the LP had a garish yellow sleeve on which the title was emblazoned. It was clumsy, vulgar, and tasteless - all the things that Malcolm McLaren would have been delighted for it to be, though utterly devoid of the high-art irony implicit in virtually everything else that had emerged from the Glitterbest camp: one felt that the group was running out of inspiration, that at best they were bored, at worst seriously in trouble.

This fear was amplified by what the album contained - a serious dearth of new material. Furthermore, although the LP contained all four singles, as well as 'Submission', 'New York', and 'Bodies', it seemed somehow to be a mess: no-one expected a Sex Pistols album to be a 'pleasant' listening experience, but they certainly expected more than the trashy shock-horror-outrage of much of it.

An eight-foot-high poster was available as point-of-sale material. And this poster version of the album sleeve packed the display windows of Virgin's nationwide chain of record stores. One might have expected such overkill from Virgin, but it was also a response to the refusal of the three major

British chains of record retailers – Woolworth, WH Smith, and Boots – to handle the record.

On the day of release the manager of the Virgin shop in Nottingham was arrested for obscenity – it was the word 'bollocks' that caused all the trouble.

It was like a gift. Seizing the moment, Virgin and McLaren manipulated the imminent court case, squeezing every inch of publicity from it.

The trial was on 24 November. For the Pistols, Virgin had employed the services of John Mortimer QC, the celebrity barrister who doubles as a best-selling author. Citing historic literary usage of the term 'bollocks', Mortimer made mince-meat of the prosecution charge. The jury retired for only twenty minutes before deciding that the group had not been acting indecently.

That weekend the country was littered with record stores with window displays of the 'Bollocks' album cover.

This public triumph concealed a private tragedy. Sid Vicious's heroin habit was making him virtually uncontrollable. He was also prey to all manner of internal demons. On 30 November, Sid got immensely out-of-it and tried to commit suicide by jumping from the window of the Ambassador Hotel in Bayswater. Nancy Spungen only just managed to save her lover, grabbing onto his belt as he attempted to plunge to the pavement. Sid expressed his gratitude by kicking the shit out of her, a noisy *contretemps* that led to their arrest, when the police arrived, for possession of illegal substances – no charges were formally proffered.

Sid's relationship with Nancy was causing the rest of the group deep concern and worry. It seemed to be one of those 'difficult' relationships.

Even the mild Paul Cook was still suffering the slights of outrageous fortune: in an interview in the *Daily Mail* his mother declared that she didn't want him back in the house. She was 'making a nice little dining room out of Paul's bedroom,' she said.

Mrs Cook also had a thing or two to say about that there Johnny Rotten. 'After he'd been around a bit, I used to tell my husband that it wasn't surprising he couldn't find any pins to eat his winkles because Johnny Rotten had taken them all. We all had a say in calling him Johnny Rotten, because his teeth were all green and decayed.'

And everyone was playing the McLaren game. On 9 November, for example, Stiff deleted Ian Dury's instant classic 'Sex And Drugs And Rock And Roll', an act very much in the spirit of the times, yet another of the endless scams being perpetrated that year to glamorise the artistic integrity of various artists. For the record (as it were), Stiff claimed that they had no warehouse space for back stock; and that the company was only interested in new records, not in being a museum – more slick marketing dressed up as hipper-than-thou 'street' wisdom.

Generation X's management were also playing sub-McLaren games – almost ten years later, Tony James would attempt to outdo McLaren with the launch of Sigue Sigue Sputnik on an intitially successful but ultimately misconceived tidal wave of 'designer violence'. Now, however, on 18 November they had a new single released, 'Wild Youth/Wild Dub', a potential 'teen' anthem of the sort with which Duran Duran would be more successful five years later. A story went out that, despite being credited as 'Wild Dub', a number of the records featured a different tune entitled 'No No No'. This seemed a transparently obvious, and somewhat limp-wristed attempt by the group to try and wring sales from their relatively unproven market.

On 17 November the Ramones had their third album released, 'Rocket To Russia'. This seemed to be the speed with which punk matters should be travelling. The first single pulled from the record was 'Rockaway Beach': in yet another version of the new marketing techniques whipped into shape by punk, the first 10,000 copies contained a free Ramones poster.

By the end of the year, a host of new acts were headlining their own major tours: the Boomtown Rats were playing at the Hammersmith Odeon, Tom Robinson was topping the bill at the Lyceum, Ian Dury was playing the Top Rank circuit of ballrooms. Suddenly a whole load of new groups were very big indeed.

In the middle of December, meanwhile, Elvis Costello and Nick Lowe signed to Radar Records, formed by two of England's most perceptive A& R men, Martin Davis and Andrew Lauder; they had a distribution deal via WEA, except for in the United States where they were with CBS.

There were some new instant icons. In the *NME*, for example, Sham 69 got their biggest coverage to date. 'I know I'm not gonna change the world – if I ever believed I was gonna change the world I'd be a complete nutcase,' said their singer Jimmy Pursey. 'All I can do is get out on that stage, sing about it and make people enjoy it at the same time. I'm not a politician, I'm not a leader, all I am is a bloke who gets on stage and sings rock and roll.'

The terminology had changed. Once again, 'rock and roll' was being referred to as the yardstick. In fact, from now on it was very important to be a 'rock and roller' and not someone involved with 'rock', which was now recognised as simply having been a marketing ploy to open up the album market.

'Never Mind the Bollocks' soared to the top of the UK charts, entering at number one, displacing Cliff Richard's '40 Golden Greats'. That no-one was being converted to buy the record apart from their specific fan-base was evident from the way 'Bollocks' was itself dislodged from the top slot after only two weeks by Bread's 'The Sound of Bread'.

On 5 December the group started a ten day tour of Holland. A UK tour followed on from this Dutch jaunt. It began with a Friday night show at Brunel University in Uxbridge, on London's very western perimeter. The group were powerful - paradoxically, partially because of the wilful lack of effort being put into his performance by John Lydon - but the atmosphere was poisonous, created by the visible and arrogant air of violence emanating from (a) those members of the university rugby club hired as bouncers, and (b) the increasingly pathetic and transparent onstage psychosis of Sid Vicious. There was a sense of utter internal disarray, of deep unhealthiness.

Things were in an unstoppable downward spiral. Again, dates on this UK tour were cancelled, following pressure from local police or politicians: in Aberdeen, councillor Margaret Williams opposed the Pistols playing in the city - she had heard that they cut up animals onstage and covered themselves in blood. And now the bans seemed - in the then fashionable reggae terminology - outernational. On 15 December the Pistols were denied US visas, forcing the cancellation of a planned lightning trip for an appearance on *Saturday Night Live* - to add insult to injury, they were replaced by Elvis Costello.

On 25 December the Sex Pistols played their last ever date in Britain, a party for the children of striking firemen and others who were similarly disadvantaged. In jovial spirits Lydon dived headfirst into the Christmas cake, setting off an expansive food fight. In stark contrast, after the show had ended and the children had left, Sid and Nancy were filmed in what Sid described as a 'pornographic movie'. 'You know, dominance and submission, sucking and fucking,' said Nancy.

The Sex Pistols were about to leave for the United States, their effort to conquer the largest record market in the world. A tour of both northern and southern cities had been booked. On 29 December, immediately prior to departure, the group learned that their applications for US visas had again been turned down, the assorted members' various petty criminal convictions being cited against them, John Lydon's speed bust earlier in the year weighing especially against them. Following direct interventions from the chief attorney for Warner Brothers, to whom the group had signed in the USA, this decision was reversed two days later. Having been forced to cancel the tour's early dates, the shows would now begin in Atlanta, Georgia, and continue through the south, concluding in San Francisco.

1977 was conclusively over and done with. *Investors Chronicle* nominated the Sex Pistols as 'Young Businessmen of the Year'.

The story of the Sex Pistols' only American tour, one of debacle and disaster, is well known. After the Atlanta date, at the Great South East Music Hall, on 5 January, the group played in Memphis, Tennessee, San Antonio, Texas, Baton Rouge, Louisiana, Dallas, Texas, and Tulsa, Oklahoma, before arriving in San Francisco to play the Winterland Ballroom on 14 January.

Assiduous efforts were made to keep Sid Vicious away from heroin. So successful were they that at the Longhorn Ballroom in Dallas, he came onstage with the words 'GIMME A FIX' gouged into his bare chest.

After the San Francisco show John Lydon chivvied the audience: 'Ever get the feeling you've been cheated?' Separated from the rest of the group, who were staying at a different hotel, Lydon was about to learn that he himself was on the verge of being cheated. Even before the tour, Lydon's relationship with

Rotten: 'That Brunel gig - that last London date - that was the worst gig ever. The PA didn't work. There was no bar. And they lost the key to the front door so that the audience couldn't get in.'

Rotten on last UK date: 'That was brilliant.'

Interviewer: 'It was a benefit for the striking firemen, wasn't it?'

'And orphans and things like that. Malcolm hated it. Malcolm didn't want to know. Because we lost a lot of money. Dear me. How tragic. Funny that. That gig was never mentioned in the press, was it? Yet at the time they were following us around the country. "Pistols banned here. Cause trouble there."'

Interviewer: 'Was that the gig where you dived into the Christmas cake?'

'I was pushed into it. By a load of horrible six-year-old girls. Savage beasts. That was great, that was. So good. Sid was pinching sweets from everyone; he couldn't cope at all with having kids as an audience. Just couldn't handle it. He couldn't do all that nonsense with his face and with his shirt off. It didn't wash at all. They just thought he was a buffoon. And he knew they knew. And he was.'

103

Rotten: 'I think he [McLaren] did things to the best of his abilities. He didn't start out for the wrong reasons. It's just that money interfered. He gets things wrong and he tries to manipulate people's lives like it's a game of chess. It was quite absurd because my whole attitude towards the Pistols was "This is going to be an honest band." But he was working against it.

'It started out as a laugh, right? Being asked to sing in a band!?! I just thought "Whoopee. Ha-ha. What fun. A bumpkin like me who can hardly be bothered to talk." And then I took myself a little serious. And I found I wasn't scared shitless of yelling in a microphone and it was really good fun. And 'cos they couldn't write words I did all that - all the literature. It suited me fine; all the things I'd wanted to moan about all my measly life I got out in songs. Whoopeeee...'

Rotten: 'It got to be a joke, didn't it? It just got stagnant. That year when we didn't do anything...We never did any new songs, nothing. No-one could be bothered. There was no point. That's what messed it up. I've got nothing against playing live. I just don't want to do it night after night.'

Malcolm McLaren had broken down almost entirely - due to the singer's bid to escape the manipulations of his manager's cod artrage games. And the pressures of the American dates had only increased the sense of mutual loathing between the pair.

Although the Pistols had a tour of Sweden scheduled, to begin on 19 January, immediately after the US dates, McLaren insisted that the group fly to Rio de Janeiro in Brazil, to film a sequence for the film that had become his obsession.

There was the problem of a genuinely practical nature: how could the exhausted group possibly fly from California to Brazil and arrive in Sweden in sufficient time for their tour? But what Lydon found especially repugnant was that McLaren planned to film the group with Ronnie Biggs, the almost legendary - in Britain, anyway - escaped Great Train Robber: there was no extradition treaty between Britain and Brazil. The Great Train Robbery had taken place outside London in August 1963, the biggest theft of money in the country up to that date. In the course of the hold-up, the driver had been beaten about the head, dying some years later as a consequence of the blows. For years afterwards Lydon would obsessively wax outrage at the idea that the group should be involved with the perpetrator of the poor man's death. However, it wasn't Biggs who coshed the man, and his role in the robbery had been relatively minor. All the same, McLaren's idea was crass and tacky, and almost as devoid of inspiration as the 'Bollocks' album cover.

Sid Vicious had performed the San Francisco show on heroin, the only gig before which he had managed to make a junkie connection. For the next two days he was able to indulge himself in this favourite and ultimately lethal pastime. Political manoeuvrings worthy of a Renaissance court were meanwhile taking place between McLaren and Lydon, who had not been informed that the group were due to depart for Rio early on the morning of 15 January.

Sid was therefore free the next day to OD on smack and be rushed to hospital. On the morning of 17 January, Paul Cook and Steve Jones finally left the United States on a flight to Rio de Janeiro. John Lydon took a plane to New York, to stay with *NME* photographer Joe Stevens. Sid remained in hospital; once released he overdosed again, on methadone on a flight to New York, where he was again hospitalised. 'I'm sick of working with the Sex Pistols,' Lydon told the *New York Post*. The Sex Pistols were over.

Almost as soon as he got off the plane back to London Sid Vicious gave an interview to the writer of this book for the *NME*; it was simultaneously filmed for the documentary *DOA*. The director Lech Kowalski had followed the Pistols' tour, accompanied by the man bankrolling his movie project, Tom Forcade, the publisher of *High Times* magazine. (Riven with perhaps

understandable paranoia, John Lydon would insist that Forcade and Kowalski had CIA connections – there was simply no truth in this whatsoever.) As he lay on a bed in his west London mews cottage, with Nancy Spungen next to him, Sid's vocal chords were so destroyed by a combination of drug abuse and sickness that his voice really did sound much of the time like a death rattle – as though this was some wonderful stroke of deeply ironic McLaren-like symbolism.

In the course of the interview – in between falling asleep on Nancy several times and accidentally stubbing cigarettes out on her leg – a smacked-out Sid revealed something of the managerial-client financial status between McLaren and the Pistols. For example, although the seven-year lease on the mews cottage in which he and Nancy were ensconced was bought with Sid's money, it had been put in the name of the much regarded Sophie Richmond, McLaren's erstwhile secretary. Furthermore, although the group were at no point on more than £60 a week, they would be bought whatever they desired in the form of stereos or colour TVs – the kind of condescension that was a cliché of old-school pop group management, often masking sinister motivation.

Sid, however, appeared to have swallowed lock, stock and barrel the McLaren line on John Lydon, once one of his closest friends and the man who had brought him into the Pistols. They had met at college in Hackney in the spring of 1974, when Sid was still known by his real name of John Simon Ritchie. At the time Lydon had long hair that he sometimes dyed blue and sometimes green; he had been renowned for his withering sarcasm. As should have been the case with a Bowie freak, John Ritchie's hair was coloured red. Lydon had named him 'Sid' after a pet hamster that he owned.

Sid and Nancy – who hadn't been in America with the 'bass-player' – were complaining that on the American tour Lydon had begun to behave 'like Rod Stewart'. In fact, this description came from Malcolm McLaren, one of the typically English divide-and-rule tactics of the 'situationist'. And the comparison was especially inaccurate; its source was a characteristically uninspired attempt, by a Burbank Warner Brothers executive, at pigeon-holing Lydon's hairstyle. The only note of compassion and understanding for his former friend came from a comment from Sid that since John Lydon had been attacked in London six months previously, he had grown increasingly paranoid, insisting on being surrounded by 'thirty people' when he went out – yet Sid even managed to turn such understandable fear into a criticism.

In hindsight, the interview reads chillingly. In particular Nancy Spungen's request for Sid to be poured only a small brandy: 'Sid's not supposed to drink. Otherwise he'll die.'

Just a small segment of the interview provides the tone.

Reporter: 'Sid, perhaps you could expand on what was written in last week's Thrills [*a section of the NME*] where it was said that you and Malcolm both decided you'd had enough of the band on a car ride out to San Francisco airport. Perhaps you could say exactly what it was that decided you on that.'

Sid: (pause) 'What was the question again? I'm sorry. I'm really tired.'

Nancy: 'Sid! WAKE UP, willya. You gave the guy an interview AND NOW YOU'RE FUCKING SLEEPING!'

Sid: 'You know, I said to you "If this American tour doesn't work out..."I decided that...' (*Sid takes a small nap*).

Nancy (*elbowing Sid in the ribs*): 'He told me that if John didn't straighten out on this American tour then he was going to quit.' (*A further elbowing in the ribs*). 'NOW GO ON!!!'

Sid opens his mouth in the shape of assorted words several times.

Nancy: 'We can't understand a word you're saying, Sid. Take some of that cough syrup.' (*To me*) 'He's got a really bad throat. He's been very sick.'

Sid musters his energies (*almost pleadingly*): 'Well, do you know what I mean? Well, you tell him.'

A few minutes later Sid announces, almost in tears: 'I'm so glad I'm out of that group.'

In the *NME* Top Ten the week of that interview, the Pistols' album was at number nine. However, the rest of the Top Ten gave no sign whatsoever of the seething social disruption throughout the UK. Fleetwood Mac's 'Rumours' was solidly lodged at number one. Apart from the Pistols, the rest of the Top Ten album chart, in descending order, was 'Abba the Album', 'Sound of Bread', Donna Summer's 'Greatest Hits', Rod Stewart's 'Footloose and Fancy Free', Elton John's 'Greatest Hits Volume 2', Tammy Wynette's '20 Country Classics', a K-Tel compilation entitled 'Disco Fever', and Electric Light Orchestra's 'Out of the Blue'. The only hint of punk activity came in the number twenty-five position, with Ian Dury's 'New Boots and Panties'.

But there was also now another world altogether, dominated by the indie labels that had sprung up, a consequence both of the formation of Stiff Records and of the Buzzcocks' 'Spiral Scratch' EP: new garden shed independent labels blossomed every week.

And from the acts signed to major labels, there was also constant activity. At the beginning of January, Sham 69 had released 'There's Gonna Be A Borstal Breakout'. The same month Glen Matlock's Rich Kids had their eponymously titled debut single in the shops, supported by a series of gigs.

And at Surrey Sound in Leatherhead, the Police were recording their first album. Their singer, Sting, would later describe the punk springboard off which the trio leapt as having been a 'flag of convenience'.

The Police's cooption of reggae's hypnotic beat was eventually to play a large part in making Sting's addictive songs into such enormous international hits that by 1982 they had become the biggest group in the world.

They were, of course, reviled by punk purists, all part of the utter lack of solidarity between the participants in the movement. Frankly, the endless mutual slagging off was tedious, self-righteous, frequently embarrassing and at a very low level. And everyone seemed to play this particularly petty game. The-Jam-slag-off-the-Clash-the-Clash-slag-off-the-Stranglers-John-Lydon-slags-off-anyone-he-can-think-of-everyone-slags-off-the-Police.

Rotten on Sid: 'His attitude changed completely when he met Nancy. One hundred per cent. He was banging up all day and night. He became a total bore and just didn't recognise anyone anymore. It was pathetic. He can't play the bass. He never really could. It was horrible the noise he used to get out of it, about the most offensive racket ever.

'The reputation he got for himself as a bass player....Johnny Thunders - now you know what he's like. He's out of his box - refused to let Sid jam with him because he thinks Sid is so appalling it's not worth talking about. I thought that was so funny - one junkie being discerning about another.'

Interviewer: 'But it's true that you got him into the Pistols?'

'Yeah.'

Interviewer: 'But you knew he couldn't play then, presumably?'

'No, but he was alright then. He was learning and learning fast. And then he just got really fucked up. You've seen him go from bad to worse. I've seen him go from good to bad to worse.'

Interviewer: 'That must have been quite depressing.'

'Just morbid. It fitted in with everything else. Everything else was falling apart so I didn't see why that shouldn't.'

Rotten on Sid's plight: 'I was fucking annoyed. I'd seen the way his old dear and Malcolm had carved him up - that whole scene whereby they got him out of prison to record a few tracks. He had no fucking hope. Now I was willing to get a lawyer and go over to New York and sort out his problems but Sid's old dear wouldn't talk to me 'cos Malcolm told her not to.'

Wasn't there something very Stalinist about all this mutual denouncing? If it had been a real grown-up (sic) revolution, shouldn't we have run for our lives from these self-appointed cultural guardians?

Mick Jones of the Clash was one of the few punk musicians who largely refused to play the game of mutual back-stabbing. Not only was he part of the foundations of the movement, but he was also extremely perceptive. 'If you criticise other groups in the media, you're only drawing attention to the same faults in yourself,' he told me, in 1977, was one of his ground-rules.

Seeking the source of their inspiration, Jones and Joe Strummer had taken a trip to Jamaica in November, 1977. At the time the island was in a desperate state. Michael Manley's policy of allying not with the United States but with other Third World countries, especially Cuba, had had disastrous consequences, not the least of which was a policy of destabilisation put into force by the CIA. Political gunmen, the forerunners of the Jamaican drug posses that would later blight the United States, ran rampant. A team of government-backed hitmen, the Eradication Squad, attempted to counter this. Even in uptown Kingston the sound of gunshots was a daily occurrence.

For Jones and Strummer to land in the midst of this purgatorial maelstrom wearing the Clash's characteristic multi-zippered military-like fatigues was only guaranteed to add to the confusion. Or at least to their own. Checking into the Pegasus hotel in New Kingston, they ventured out to look for fellow musicians....But could find none, not even Lee 'Scratch' Perry, the producer of 'Complete Control'. In Jamaica, of course, all facts are highly subjective, even such things as people's addresses. After wandering down to the city's dockside area, they scored a large amount of 'herb', and retired to their hotel rooms. 'We fuckin' went out on the streets dressed to the nines,' said Strummer. 'We thought we'd show 'em where it was at. 'Cos they all like looking sharp, too. Boy, we got some funny looks. Sometimes when it got a bit heavy we'd pass ourselves off as merchant seamen.' Sufficiently inspired by their giant bag of ganja, they wrote much of the group's next album, notably the driving opening song, 'Safe European Home', with its decidedly non-PC observations: '*I went to the place where every white face/is an invitation to robbery*'. This song – one of their greatest ever – had over sixty lines, before it was stripped down to a third of that.

At the time that the Pistols were imploding a couple of months later, Joe Strummer was heading for his own personal crisis. It was not unknown in that time for the Clash singer to be found around London in all manner of out-of-it states – being discovered lying drunk in the gutter outside Dingwalls with rain-water washing into his mouth, for example. And the consequences of such an unhealthy lifestyle came to a head in February of 1978: Joe Strummer was hospitalised for eleven days with hepatitis.

That same month John Lydon, shellshocked from the break-up of the Pistols, also found himself on a plane to Jamaica, thereby cementing and confirming the notion of the punk-reggae alliance of outsiders. The trip was instigated by Virgin boss Richard Branson, who was on a reggae signing spree. In this, Lydon's knowledge of the music was essential, and he would watch as the cream of Kingston's musicians trouped through the lobby of the Sheraton hotel down to Branson's poolside cabana. Then he would go off and smoke chalices of ganja with U Roy.

Somewhere within these clouds of smoke he seemed to find his life's path forward – *Yes Future!* It was to be called Public Image Ltd, an ironic group name that made a comment on the (literally?) lethal media overkill that had destroyed the Pistols. In various forms it was to last for the next fifteen years.

In March 1978, with Strummer released from hospital under doctor's orders not to drink alcohol for the next six months, thus helping him lose a building beer belly, the Clash released a new single, 'Clash City Rockers', self-referential in the manner of many reggae tunes.

At the end of the month, on 30 March, there took place one of the more distasteful episodes in the group's career. Paul Simonon and Topper Headon were arrested at Rehearsal Rehearsals, where they were practising songs for their next album. Trying out an airgun that a friend was offering to sell to them, they had gone up to the studio's roof and blasted away at some pigeons, housed in coops by the adjacent railway track. They killed three of them.

Only when a police helicopter and armed CID officers arrived on the scene, did the Clash discover that (a) the pigeons were expensive racing birds, and (b) the police had assumed this to be an act of terrorism by the 'anti-establishment' group. The fact that it was more like a prank by the less aware elements of the gang led by William Brown, the Richmal Crompton creation, did not prevent Simonon and Headon being lodged overnight in Brixton prison and subsequently given substantial fines.

Never one to lose an opportunity to turn things to their advantage, the Clash wrote a song about the incident for their next album; 'Guns on the Roof' turned this episode of extraordinarily petty stupidity – which appalled Mick Jones – into one of pseudo-heroism.

A month later, on 30 April, the group performed in a rather more elevated role, at the first major concert organised by Rock Against Racism, a new organisation that had sprung out of the rise of the right-wing National Front in the UK. Had the hard-left politicos who dominated the organisation, the kind who had always despised rock'n'rollers, suddenly become converted to the music through punk's egalitarian ethos? There were those who were deeply suspicious of their motivation.

On a Sunday afternoon in Hackney's Victoria Park, after a march that had begun at Trafalgar Square, the Clash played to a crowd of 80,000 people. For the sake of solidarity, they forsook the characteristic rock'n'roll ego battles over bill-topping, and gave way to the Boomtown Rats – the bill also included the Tom Robinson Band and Steel Pulse, the reggae group from Birmingham who had played a large part in the punk-reggae alliance. A blistering performance by the Clash was rendered even more notable by their being joined onstage by Jimmy Pursey, Sham 69's man-of-the-people singer, for the last numbers, including the inevitable – and, especially in the circumstances, inevitably controversial – 'White Riot'. Controversy lurked

Rotten on the PiL *raison d'etre*: 'That's one thing we've all got in common. We all hate rock'n'roll.'

Public Image Ltd (PiL) was not the only name considered by the new John Rotten combo: the Royal Family, the Carnivorous Butterflies, and the Future Features were also considered.

Rotten: 'One of the first things I was ever quoted as saying was "I'd like to see more bands like us." Right? When I said that, I didn't mean exactly that. Unfortunately that's what happened. Imitations. Billions of them. And I wanted nothing to do with any of them. There were a few originals, but not many. They were all outnumbered by the crud. I didn't want to be anything to do with it.'

Rotten: 'I'm not doing anything that anyone else couldn't do...unless they didn't want to do it.'

Rotten: 'I can do what any genius can do (laughs). As simple as that.'

beneath this Clash appearance, however. Their appearing on the bill had been at the insistence of Mick Jones; backstage at the event Bernie Rhodes told all who would listen that he had been vehemently against the group playing in the concert at all. Trouble was brewing.

Just over two months later, at the beginning of July, the Clash released perhaps their greatest ever single, '(White Man) In Hammersmith Palais'. The story of a reggae show that Strummer had gone to, the song slowed down the by now characteristic 180 mph punk pace into an epic, ballad-like masterwork about the state of racial play in Britain. But despite its unquestionable merits the song only reached number 32 in the charts.

Any worries that the low chart placing might reflect a group in trouble were dispelled by their "Out On Parole" tour, a ten-date sprint around Britain that began on Wednesday, 28 June at Friars, Aylesbury. Supporting the Clash was another group managed by Bernie Rhodes, the Specials AKA.

In Glasgow, Strummer and Simonon were arrested on 'drunk and disorderly' charges: they were not drunk and disorderly at all, and the charge was a set-up by vicious, thick local police, seemingly in collusion with the psychotic bouncers who had been hurling themselves at the audience from the stage of the Apollo. As his group was being manhandled into police vans, Bernie Rhodes was entertaining a potential American promoter who maintained he had never seen anything like the scenes he had just witnessed inside the theatre.

Rhodes was not to be entertaining such types for much longer. On 21 October, he was officially fired by the group, backed by CBS, who found him equally impossible to deal with. The diminutive and obtuse Rhodes was replaced by Caroline Coon, erstwhile punk and Clash champion and girlfriend of Paul Simonon. On 1 November Rhodes took out a court order under which all the Clash's earnings were to be paid directly to him. This was to cause hell.

By then work had been completed on the group's second album. Columbia in the USA had refused to release 'The Clash', claiming it was unpalatable to American radio. The fact that it sold 100,000 copies on import – a record – must have had some effect on their promotion of the group, however. And the Clash were also anxious to break the United States market. At the urging of the record company they had taken on Sandy Pearlman as producer – the same chore on the first album had been undertaken by Mickey Foote, the group's soundman. Pearlman was most notable for his work with Blue Oyster Cult, a vaguely postmodern heavy metal group beloved of critics.

When 'Give 'Em Enough Rope' was released on 25 November, it entered the UK chart at number two. The first album had only made number twelve, so this was a triumph, even if the record was by no means the consistent glory of its predecessor. And the Clash also finally had their first Top 20 single in 'Tommy Gun', taken from the LP.

For much of the year John Lydon had sat things out; other than a couple of interviews with the music press during the summer, a veil of silence was maintained over the progress of Public Image Ltd, as his new group was called. In May he had revealed that it consisted of former Clash guitarist Keith Levene, bass-player Jah Wobble (formerly John Wardle), and drummer Jim Walker, a Canadian who had won his place through taking part in the auditions for the position. The group's first single, 'Public Image', released in October, was a *tour de force*. It made number nine; the album from which it was taken, also

Rotten: 'I'm only twenty-two. And I feel I've seen everything. It makes it very difficult sometimes. 'I've learned a lot. I now see what's on the other side of the fence and I don't like it. But at least I know how to protect myself from it a bit better now. I won't get messed up like the last time. No-one in this business is ever going to walk on me again. I'll do the walking. I feel exceptionally strong about that.

'It's no good being nice and young and naive. There's no good in that at all. You've got to do it all yourself and you've gotta learn quick. And you can't look for sympathy either.'

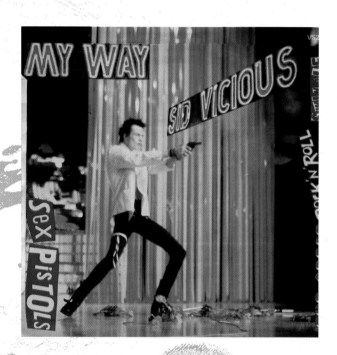

inevitably entitled 'Public Image', made number twenty-two. Their stage debut came on Christmas Day at London's Rainbow.

Lydon's artistic success, however, was somewhat overshadowed by the more aberrant activities of Sid Vicious, his erstwhile companion. Unexpectedly Sid at first had seemed to be going from strength to strength. At the beginning of April he had been in Paris, shooting material at the Olympia Theatre for the Sex Pistols film with which McLaren was still progressing, this time using the directing abilities of a young British film school graduate called Julian Temple.

On 30 June one of the fruits of this shoot was released when a group nominally known as the Sex Pistols put out 'No One is Innocent', on which the vocals were handled by Ronnie Biggs (Virgin had baulked at McLaren's insistence that the song be titled 'Cosh the Driver'), coupled with Sid's version of the standard 'My Way' – it was this side of the single that got all the airplay and became a hit. Roy Carr reviewed the record in the *NME*: 'Just a passing thought,' he wrote with chilling prescience, 'but the last person to record 'My Way' died soon after.'

To promote the record Sid played a show at London's Electric Ballroom, supported by the Vicious White Kids (Glen Matlock, Rat Scabies, and Steve New) under the banner title of Sid Sods Off. Sid literally was doing that: he was leaving to live in what he imagined was decadent rock'n'roll heaven in New York.

By the end of September he was playing the part of vocalist in a set of mostly covers at Max's Kansas City, part of the Idols, with Arthur Kane, Jerry Nolan, and Steve Dior. (Nolan had thoughtfully introduced Sid to his methadone clinic: medical staff there had been astonished by the extent of Sid's addiction.)

But then came the biggest of all the many big headlines that punk had so far produced. On 12 October Sid called the police from his room at the Chelsea hotel – someone had stabbed Nancy Spungen to death, he told them. Charged on 13 October with second degree murder, Sid was locked up in the detox unit at New York's notorious Riker's Island prison. Two days later there were T-shirts on sale in Malcolm McLaren and Vivienne Westwood's shop proclaiming 'I'M ALIVE, SHE'S DEAD, I'M YOURS'. Some felt this was the last straw in denoting the true scumbag nature of this increasingly creepy pair – their role with the Pistols was beginning to seem like that of voyeuristic child molesters.

On 17 October, Sid was released from Riker's Island after Virgin had put up bail of $50,000. Six days later he tried to commit suicide by ingesting all of his available methadone supply. Recovered, he made the Manhattan scene for a while. But on 7 December Sid got into a fight with Todd, brother of Patti Smith, who he slashed with a bottle before being hauled off once again to Riker's, for violation of his bail terms.

Rotten on Sid's death: 'It wasn't a shock when he was killed, and I know who I blame though I'm not gonna be so stupid as to say it. But it was pretty obvious he was given a hot shot. Is that what they call it when they lace it up with everything from arsenic to boot polish? He was a fool. Fell for it.'

Rotten on McLaren: 'Let's just say that if Malcolm breathes it's too much for me to stomach.'

Sting: 'We got in through the back door in 1977. We weren't the real thing. Andy's age quickly gave everything away. But the revolution was upon us, and you had to pick sides. I thought, Well, I'm certainly not going to go with the Genesis mob - I'll go with something I actually agree with. And although in the initial stages I didn't really get off on the Sex Pistols' music, the attitude was so compelling I had to side with that lot.

'I was into serious music. I didn't even listen to rock music...I never listened to Led Zeppelin or anyone like that. I could never stand those groups. In fact, to me the Sex Pistols sound was very much an extension of that. However, it was the verbalising that went round it that really struck me.

'But then I really *did* get into the Sex Pistols, and my favourite album for a whole year was "Never Mind the Bollocks". It was so heavy. Paul Cook was a formidable drummer.

'It was the same for Stewart in Curved Air. They weren't happening then, and when the Sex Pistols came along, they knew they weren't going to happen again: a tidal wave came along and you had to either dive in or be drowned.

'We were in a curious position. Because of how old we were, and the experiences we'd had, we could be fairly objective about the whole thing. I could see that punk was going to develop in some way. It was going to have to ameliorate. It was obvious that if you could ally that energy and that drive to a more musical form, it would be dynamite. And what I wanted to have was energy rock'n'roll allied to harmonic, melodic music.

'What I started off doing was structuring songs that had an eight-bar section of rock'n'roll coupled with, say, sixteen bars of reggae. Which, in fact, you can see in "Roxanne". And through listening to the various songs you can see how my writing gradually became more sinuous. There's a reggae element in "Don't Stand so Close to Me", but you can hardly hear it. The music flows more now - there's hardly any breaks. Initially, though, it was just very crudely obvious that if you joined the two together you'd get something else.'

Sting on his first recordings with the Police: 'I just went along with them and sang them as hard as I could. No, it wasn't false punk. I mean, what's a real punk. Our first record was entirely a tribute to Stewart's energy and focus. The band wouldn't have happened without him.'

In other non–Pistols and non–Clash punk news in 1978:

In April Siouxsie And The Banshees had broken audience attendance records at London's Music Machine, an extraordinary feat for an unsigned group - at the end of August, they finally struck a recording deal, with Polydor; and another group with a female vocalist, Blondie, hit the number 2 spot in the UK charts with Denis. At the end of April Elvis Costello released his next single, Pump It Up, only two months since I Don't Want To Go To Chelsea had come out. (Records were being released at a furious pace, with colossal idealism behind this return to the singles standard.) The B-side was an album outtake with Mick Jones guesting on guitar.

Meanwhile, Angels With Dirty Faces, the second single from Sham 69 hit the shops and the charts, something of a counterpoint to a wacky French punk piece - Ca Plane Pour Moi, by Plastic Bertrand, an off-the-wall hit.

At the end of May, The Members released Solitary Confinement on the One Off label, a Stiff offshoot. Consisting of vocalist Nicky Tesco, lead guitarist Nigel Bennett, guitarist Jean-Marie Carroll, bass-player Chris Payne, and drummer Adrian Lillywhite, the group were to hit the charts the next year on Virgin with Sounds Of The Suburbs.

In June Riffraff had their debut single out on Chiswick: I Wanna Be a Cosmonaut / Romford Girls / What's The Latest / Sweet As Pie. Their singer and songwriter was called Billy Bragg. A month later Talking Heads had their second album released: More Songs About Buildings And Food, produced by Brian Eno at Compass Point. It sold many more copies than the Riffraff record.

A few days later The Jam had A Bomb In Wardour Street in the shops, (un)inspired by The Vortex. On August 18 The Rich Kids released their first album, Ghosts Of Princes In Towers. When Public Image didn't show for a recording of the pop TV programme Revolver - they had gone off for the day to the seaside at Camber Sands instead - they were ironically replaced by The Rich Kids. The same month Manchester "punk poet" John Cooper Clarke signed to CBS: his first single was Post-War Glamour Girl / Kung Fu International.

These pictures were taken during the tour to promote 'Join Hands', the second LP from Siouxsie And The Banshees.

The group consisted of Siouxsie, Steve Severin, guitarist John McKay, and drummer Kenny Morris. The line-up was extremely wobbly. After several dates, the band were due to attend a promotional signing in a Glasgow record store. Morris and McKay failed to show, however.

On returning to their hotel, Nils Stevenson, their manager, discovered they had fled, leaving pillows stuffed in their beds to resemble sleeping figures. They were not seen again for several weeks.

Robert Smith of The Cure, a friend of the group, temporarily took over duties on guitar; and Budgie joined on drums.

Lene Lovich, Mickey Jupp, Jona Lewie, and Rachel Sweet. Although Dave Robinson was a ceaseless worker and slogger, his campaigns began to seem as though they were forcing the inspiration; this belief was only sustained by the special train rented to take the Stiff Tour '78 around Britain.

Meanwhile, Manchester's Slaughter And The Dogs brought in a new singer, an inveterate writer to the letters pages of the music press called Steven Morrisey, formerly the vocalist with The Nosebleeds - although he had never turned up for an audition, he had been one of the few people who had replied to the Melody Maker ads run by Mick Jones and Tony James for London SS.

On September 27 Sham 69 played a secret gig at the Canning Town Bridge House as "The Harry All Stars" - a trailer for their next single, Hurry Up Harry, a kind of pub singalong tune that would bring Jimmy Pursey's group their biggest hit and their greatest loss of credibility. At the end of the month The Boomtown Rats released Rat Trap, which would hit number 1. Early in October The Undertones, from Londonderry, signed to Sire.

In the middle of October, The Gang Of Four released their first single, Damaged Goods. And The Stranglers were still being jolly wilful punk rockers: at Surrey University, where they were to record a show for BBC TV's Rock Goes To College series (The Police broke in the UK off this programme), the group memebrs became furious on hearing that tickets had only been given out to students: after fifteen minutes they trashed their equipment and walked offstage - on camera. Punk rock - phew! Recently the group was alleged to have broken down the door of a Top Of The Pops dressing-room. Surrey university now circulated other colleges advising them not to book The Stranglers.

On October 20, the Police began their first tour of the United States, playing 23 shows in 27 days, starting at CBGBs. Their Outlandos D'Amour album had been released four days before.

People were getting records out at a terrific pace. The Undertones had Teenage Kicks in the charts, Blondie made number 5 in the UK with Hanging On The Telephone, The Jam were in the charts again with their All Mod Cons album. Joe Jackson released his first single, Is She Really Going Out With Him? Siouxsie And The Banshees finally had their first album out, The Scream. And at the end of November Ian Dury released another classic, 'Hit Me With Your Rhythm Stick'.

In September Les Punks, consisting of Rat Scabies, Dave Vanian, Captain Sensible, and Motorhead's Lemmy played a one-off show at the Electric. The same month Stiff, whose scams by now were becoming almost tediously predictable, re-released the label's first ten singles in a box, and immediately deleted them. And on October 6, Stiff put out five new albums, one from each of the acts on the Stiff Tour '78 - Wreckless Eric,

This was the session for the EP 'Wild Things', the first record from the Creatures, a Banshees spin-off group, featuring only Siouxsie and drummer Budgie. Contemporaneously, bass-player Steve Severin was working on 'The Glove', a neo-psychedelic project with Robert Smith: this resulted in an album entitled 'Blue Sunshine'.

Budgie had joined Siouxsie And The Banshees from the Slits. As is obvious from this session, he and Siouxsie were also forging a personal relationship. The pictures were taken in a hotel in Newcastle-upon-Tyne: that afternoon Siouxsie And The Banshees had performed a show in the hotel for an audience of mentally handicapped children. That evening, Siouxsie and Budgie disappeared into the bathroom with art director Rob O'Connor and photographer Adrian Boot. When the session began, Steve Severin and guitarist John McGeogh went to the cinema to watch Clash Of The Titans.

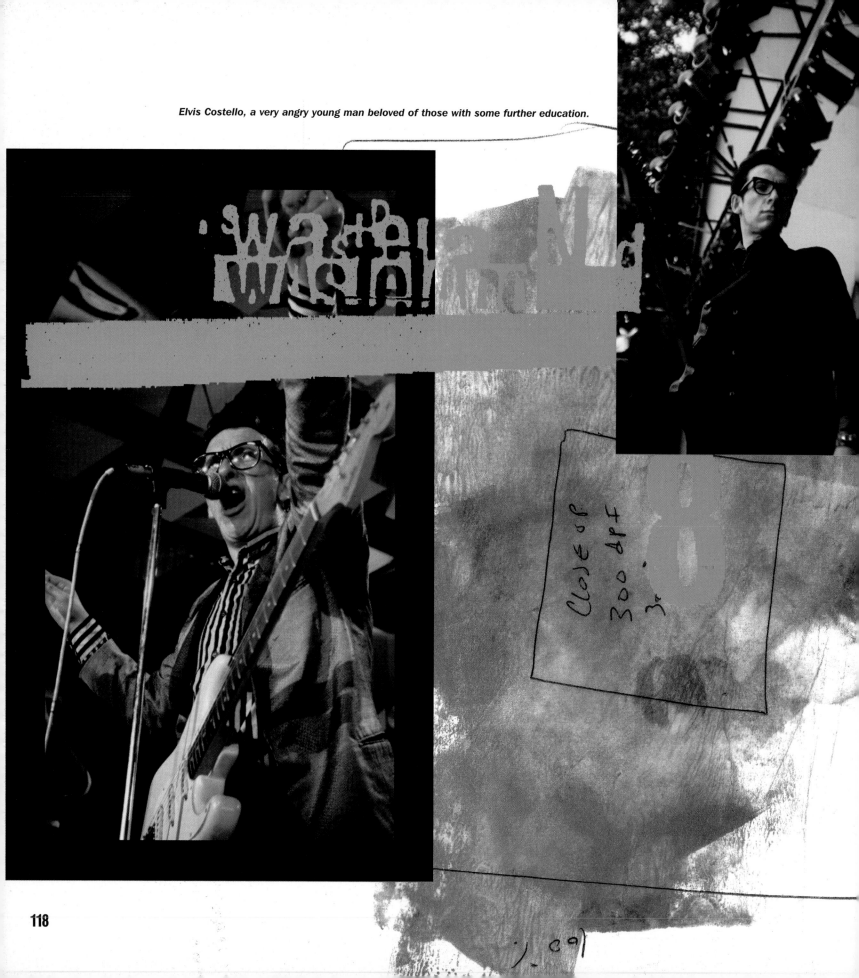

Elvis Costello, a very angry young man beloved of those with some further education.

1979 got underway in January's traditionally gloomy manner.
Released in the first week of the year, Elvis Costello's new LP 'Armed Forces' was in the shops: the previous month he had played seven nights at London's Dominion Theatre, less than two years since the release of his first single. With such a loyal fan-base it was hardly surprising that 'Armed Forces' became a number two record.

As a counterpoint to Costello's second major label excursion, the most grassroots form of punk saw expression later in the month through the release of 'The Feeding of the 5,000', the first record by Crass. Living communally in the Essex countryside, Crass were the original 'crustie' group: their hardcore idealism was at odds with their gentle nature – as was the case with many punk acts, their true stance was more like that of hippies with short hair. Almost inevitably, in the manner of so many things punk, the Irish pressing-plant took offence at one of the songs, 'Asylum', the EP's opener. Accordingly, the record opened with two minutes of silence, entitled 'Free Speech'.

In complete contrast, Generation X – who now seemed to be being marketed as the teenybop face of punk – had their second album out, 'Valley of the Dolls' – it had been tentatively titled 'Intercourse (Old Meets New)'. It was produced by Ian Hunter, the leader of Mott the Hoople which had been such an influence on, first, Mick Jones and then his friend Tony James. The trailer single was 'King Rocker', a title that was beginning to take on distinctly ironic undertones.

For although their singles had all been minor hits, Generation X seemed in trouble. No punk group was more reviled by its fellow travellers, especially since the conscious efforts at aiming the group at young girl fans. Now audiences were turning against them. In the case of Generation X 'appreciative' spit was certainly not that. The gob that would hurtle in sheets at the group seemed inspired more by loathing. Pretty Billy Idol was the principal target. At one notable, badly attended show at the Electric Ballroom, he seemed almost in tears onstage, as though he was going through such a crisis of confidence that he was on the verge of a nervous breakdown. Wasn't it increasingly clear that there was no future for him whatsoever?

The real thing, meanwhile, or the thing who thought he was the real thing, was in even bigger trouble. On 1 February John Simon Ritchie – Sid Vicious – was released from Riker's Island, where he had been in the detoxification wing since having broken his terms of bail through his assault on Patti Smith's brother. Various alleged 'friends' had arranged a supply of heroin for him on his release. Though his eyes were empty, hollow with Nancy's loss, Sid's veins were now clean. By the time of the party that was thrown for him that evening, he had already banged up an armful of smack. After the party, Sid did even more heroin.

From the note that was found by his corpse, it would seem he was consciously trying to kill himself through an overdose. 'We had a death pact,' it read. 'I have to keep my half of the bargain. Please bury me next to my baby in my leather jacket, jeans and motorcycle boots. Goodbye.'

After five years of trying, Adam Ant did very well indeed in his guise of punk pirate.

After years of penniless living in squats, Chrissie Hynde found great success with the Pretenders. The group consisted of bassist Pete Farndon, guitarist James Honeyman-Scott, and drummer Martin Chambers. Honeyman-Scott and Farndon died drug-related deaths within less than twelve months, the guitarist in June 1982 and the bass-player in April 1983.

Pretenders

Even this talk of death pacts may not have been true, however: before he had been sent back to Riker's, Sid told a friend that Nancy's death had occurred when they had been fooling around with knives; in 'fun' (sic) he had lunged at her with a blade, only meaning to cut her a little bit – *PUNK ROCK, mate!*

A week later, on 7 February, the first of the Jarndyce and Jarndyce-like legal battles between J Lydon and M McLaren got underway in the High Court in London, Sid's corpse hovering spectrally over the proceedings. These legal battles would not be finally resolved for another eight years, with substantial financial settlements – around a million pounds between them – for Lydon, Steve Jones, Paul Cook, and Sid's estate.

The Jam: Paul Weller, Bruce Foxton, Rick Buckler.

The same month the *NME* readers' poll showed conclusively the changes wrought seemingly irrevocably by punk. The Clash won the award for best group, closely followed by the Jam and the Boomtown Rats. The Jam's 'All Mod Cons' was album of the year, with the Clash's 'Give 'em Enough Rope' coming in second. At number four was 'The Scream' by Siouxsie and the Banshees, Elvis Costello's 'This Year's Model' following behind. The only sign of dissension from this pack of Young Turks by the paper's readers was the album at number three – Thin Lizzy's 'Live and Dangerous', a perfect live record whose success also reflected leader Phil Lynott's shrewd straddling of the old and new waves.

With Sid dead, and Lydon and McLaren in court, however, the future of punk seemed somewhat academic. What had been achieved had been achieved. Now nothing would be the same; the profound shift had taken place. But, as had been perhaps predicted by the ceaseless squabbling between the movement's leading contenders, there was now only to be endless diversity – though on a far higher plane than previously.

By the end of 1979 there were two main new strands, each with their own haircuts and uniforms, one a little more successful than the other. In the middle of the previous year, when out playing the On Parole tour, Joe Strummer had admitted to stepping backwards through the Jamaican music he loved to ska, the galloping, largely instrumental sound that had roughly coincided with the island's independence. Perhaps this was unsurprising: opening the show, and having a miserable time of finding sleeping accommodation, was a group from Coventry calling itself the Special AKA (who quickly became known as the Specials), another set of Bernie Rhodes' protegees. The musical speciality of the Special AKA was ska.

By the next April this group, under the supervision of its inspired

Paul Weller in March, 1979: 'I suppose most, no all, of the groups went back on what they sort of threatened in 1976, and from this point of view you can't blame them. You just don't realise what you're getting into.' By the time they disbanded at the end of 1982, the Jam were the biggest group in the UK that punk had thrown up, except for the Police. But they meant nary a light in the USA.

Paul Weller in March, 1979: 'I'm still pretty sickened by the rock business. There's still so much of that superstar shit all the way through it – getting away with murder when they ain't released a good record for years. You've got to stay dead accessible or you're finished.'

36

36A

Jerry Dammers on 2-Tone: 'It isn't necessarily just a ska thing...What we want to do is develop ska into something almost unrecognisable in much the same way as the Stones did with R&B in the '60s...We're trying to maintain the identity of the label in the way that Stax or Tamla had an identity. The basic thing is Anglo-Jamaican music. It's trying to integrate those two. But there's also soul. Especially northern soul, 'cause it's got that really strong beat... the next thing is going to be to try and integrate that with ska. One of the basic ideas behind the label is that when you have three or four bands working together on something, then they are stronger in a group than they would be as individual bands.'

leader Jerry Dammers, had not only released their first single, but had the record out on their own label, 2-Tone, distributed through Rough Trade. The A-side was a song called 'Gangsters', a re-working of the Prince Buster classic 'Al Capone'. On the flip was a tune by another act altogether, the Selecter with a number called precisely that: 'The Selecter', the Jamaican term for sound system record spinners. 'Gangsters' was an immediate success. The cartoon rude boy – Walt Jabsco, as he was known – drawn for the label, moreover, helped establish the look of the movement: tight-fitting mohair suits and porkpie hats, as worn some fifteen years previously by both Jamaican immigrant rude boys and British Mods – thus dovetailing with the Mod revival, a further new tribal movement, partially set in train by the Jam and the publicity around the filming of *Quadrophenia*, the Who's epic Mod story. (The image of Walt Jabsco was based on the picture of Peter Tosh on 'The Wailin' Wailers', the classic Studio One LP on which the Wailers were backed by the Skatalites.)

Distinctly within the context of punk's D-I-Y spirit, the sound of 2-Tone had clearly been floating out in the collective unconscious, just waiting to be called in and harnessed and shaped into hit material.

Some might have felt that the Specials/2-Tone Records did more to expose and eradicate petty racial squabbling in the UK than any number of self-righteous, overtly political organisations. Multi-racial British bands beaming into twelve million homes via *Top of the Pops* was an enormous cultural breakthrough – the subliminal changes that could be wrought were infinitely greater than any number of RAR badges.

Evidence of the truth of this came in the shape of the several other groups Dammers almost immediately discovered were performing similar material. In north London there was the perky and very funny Madness, formerly the North London Invaders, who would go on to become one of the UK's most successful singles groups.

But most of these new groups came from Britain's equivalent of Detroit – Birmingham and Coventry, the two cities that made up the

Jerry Dammers: 'I'm not very good at all at hustling. I really hate all that. But it just seemed that no-one else was going to do it. So I had to.'

Terry Hall, singer with the Specials: 'Punk still exists. 2-Tone was just the logical next step.'

Jerry Dammers: 'I just wanted 2-Tone to be like a little club. And if you liked the music then you became part of it – that's all.'

Jerry Dammers: 'The skinheads aren't a problem at all. They're a bit discriminated against, really. They just look a bit intimidating, that's all. It's not like a political statement when they get up onstage...It's just not true at all that if you're a skinhead you've gotta be in the National Front.'

Jerry Dammers: 'You can tell anybody that if they're into the NF or the British Movement that if they want to come to our gigs we just don't want them there. They're not welcome. If they've bought tickets, we'll...Well, we won't give them their money back, actually. We just don't want them there. They're not welcome.'

The Specials, a group of crucial cultural importance (far left: Jerry Dammers, rhythm guitarist Lynval Golding, bass-player Sir Horace Gentleman; left: toaster Neville Staples; top: singer Terry Hall).

heart of the automobile-manufacturing Midlands. Whilst Coventry had supplied the Specials and Selecter, Birmingham provided the Beat and Dexy's Midnight Runners. The same city also gave birth to UB40, whose base sound was reggae and rock steady rather than ska - determinedly independent in the finest punk example, they would gradually grow and grow until they became one of Britain's biggest exports.

2-Tone was the first grassroots British musical sub-division to emerge that had been directly influenced by punk. Established on the D-I-Y punk template, its multi-racial membership personified the punk-reggae fusion.

Successful and powerful in impact, 2-Tone suffered like punk, its parent, from paradox: why, one wondered, did racist skinheads swarm the stages of 2-Tone concerts as though its rigorously anti-racist themes were a vindication and not a condemnation of their personal philosophies?

From a very separate, but again very purist angle came the other new musical sub-division. Rockabilly was a consequence of punk's return to rock'n'roll from the excesses of rock music. Again, the Clash were in touch with this zeitgeist. At the very end of 1979 they released their third LP, 'London Calling', a remarkable step forward. A superb double album, retailing - in true Clash punk value-for-money spirit - for the price of a single LP, it was simply one of the finest long-playing records ever made, firmly justifying the Clash's reputation as probably the greatest rock'n'roll group there had ever been. In the United States 'London Calling' was not put out until the first week of 1980; thereby permitting *Rolling Stone* in 1990 to name the LP the Best Record of the 1980s.

The second song on the record was a version of Vince Taylor's 'Brand New Cadillac'. It was a classic of rockabilly. Rockabilly was music from the white South of the United States, country music with a semi-rhythm'n'blues beat performed by hillbillies like Elvis Presley, the King of Western Bop: Presley's 'Sun Sessions' LP, also one of the greatest records ever made, perfectly crystallises the sound, with its stand-up bass and brush drumstrokes - listen to the perfection of

HEY YOU! DON'T WATCH THAT. WATCH THIS! This is the heavy heavy monster sound! The nuttiest sound around! So if you've come in off the street, and you're beginning to feel the heat, you better start to move your feet to the rockiest rock steady beat! This is the nutty sound!!!! **Madness's Chas Smash introduces the group onstage.**

Other groups who owe a lot to Jerry Dammers: bottom left: *Selecter;* up and under: *Madness.*

'That's All Right Mama' and understand that this is as perfect art as anything by Picasso. (Was it any surprise that the cover of 'London Calling' was a pastiche of the first Presley LP for RCA?)

Sun Records, with its acts like Jerry Lee Lewis, Carl Perkins, even Johnny Cash, was the heart of rockabilly. But it was Presley who smashed down the floodgates, opening the way for the label and his label-mates - and for other early primal talents like Buddy Holly, Eddie Cochran, the early superb Johnny Burnette Trio.

People were buying these records by the ton in late 1979 and 1980, trekking down to Rock On Records in Camden Town and any other speciality shops that stocked them and scarfing them up. It was different from 2-Tone in that there weren't really any greatly successful rockabilly groups (Matchbox and Whirlwind came closest), except for the Stray Cats, imported from the United States for added authenticity. Rockabilly was a look and feel: a lot of black and pink, and hair that was greased and sculpted. Distinctly retro, it was also - as filtered through British art-school spirit - vaguely postmodern.

But Confederate flags abounded, provoking almost as much debate as had the punk resurrection of swastikas. Did it express southern racism? Or simply the romance of the south? Clearly, there was a big difference. Again, as had almost inevitably been the scenario with 2-Tone, the punk paradox.

Colossally successful across the globe, Debbie Harry and the group Blondie were the first proof that the United States music business required of the commercial viability of Punk. After Harry attempted to kickstart a solo career with the adventurous 'Koo Koo', produced by Nile Rodgers and Bernard Edwards, she retired in 1983 to nurse guitarist Chris Stein through a crippling, debilitating illness for the next three years.

ARMAgIDeoN TIME

GIVE IT
A SPIN

THE CLASH

WAVE BYE
BYE TO THE
BOSS

THE CLASH

9

The counterpoint to all this rather fundamentalist rootsiness was the New Romantic movement. In 1979 Steve Strange, and Rusty Egan, a former drummer with the Rich Kids who had auditioned for the Clash, founded a club, again like the Roxy in Covent Garden, called Blitz. Its mood of self-adoring ostentation may let it be seen as the beginning of the mood that would dominate the 1980s.

Out of this scene emerged Spandau Ballet, whose international success seemed more like that of a cult club band compared to the colossal worldwide sales of Duran Duran, kings of conspicuous consumption; boosted by the new medium of MTV, their enormous worldwide sales had Duran Duran's record company attempting risibly to compare them to the Beatles. This record company was EMI, for whom the Liverpudlian moptops had so successfully recorded and who had dropped the Pistols following the Bill Grundy furore.

By the time Duran Duran were being so lauded, the Clash had also become one of the biggest groups in the world – justifiably, for now they were arguably the greatest performing rock'n'roll group there had ever been.

'London Calling' had been a Top Thirty US album hit. However, with the release a year later of 'Sandinista', their fourth LP, the group had their backs against the wall. The LP was a three-record set, selling for the cost of a single album, in Britain the same five pound price-tag as its predecessor. In the UK, however, the record was critically castigated; weekly music press reviewers would be expected to digest a record in two or three days before committing their observations to print: 'Sandinista', punk's *War and Peace*, was simply too vast to be so absorbed. In fact, the record was the group's most ambitious and daring to date, featuring a wealth of material; that they were still on the cutting edge was confirmed simply by the choice of the first tune on the LP, 'Magnificent Seven', a song employing the new sound of 'rap'.

Ever since the dismissal of Bernie Rhodes late in 1978, the possibly unmanageable Clash had suffered from management problems. For the next few months their career was overseen by Caroline Coon. Coon was then replaced by the established management team of Andrew King and Peter Jenner, whose clients had varied from the early Pink Floyd to the Third Ear Band to Ian Dury and the Blockheads.

Working with Dury was Kosmo Vinyl, a crucial figure in the spreading of punk's egalitarian message – the 'Quest', as he romantically phrased it. Purist, flamboyant and very likable, Vinyl proved inspiring to the similarly romantic Clash; the four group members asked him to step into the management breach, taking over from King and Jenner. And it was under Vinyl's suzerainty that 'Sandinista' was released. The almost universal

negative reviews gutted the group, however. Strummer celebrated 31 December 1980, by playing lowkey rhythm guitar with his old friends from the 101'ers - calling themselves the Soul Survivors for the night - at the Tabernacle in Notting Hill, a few hundred yards from the Westway that the group had made so much of in their mythology.

There were rumours that things were about to come to a sticky end. How the group was saved comes, almost inevitably, in two versions. Again, almost predictably, one stars Joe Strummer; the other Mick Jones. Whichever is correct, both contain the requisite Clash poetry. Version A has Strummer running into Bernie Rhodes in a Wimpy Bar and inviting him back to run the group. Version B has Strummer threatening to leave the group unless someone is brought in to guide its progress - Jones humbles himself by going and asking Rhodes to return to manage the Clash.

Bernie Rhodes was back with the Clash by February 1981. And the group's shows at Bond's in New York were his first major statement.

The seventeen shows played by the Clash at this venue on Broadway and Times Square, Manhattan, in May and June 1981, marked a major upward turn in the status of the group. In the United States they already had hip cult band status; 'London Calling' had made the US Top Thirty albums. But from now on large-scale American stardom finally appeared. The career of the Clash may definitively be seen as pre- and post-Bond's: the Top Five success of 'Combat Rock' the next year can be traced back to this springboard. And therefore we may be able to trace to it the beginning of the end.

Now the way was set for 'Combat Rock'. Released in the summer of 1982, the fifth album from the Clash was produced by the experienced rock producer Glyn Johns, who had worked with the Rolling Stones and Who amongst others. A tight, twelve-song record, the first single off the LP was 'Know Your Rights', a little worryingly agit-prop and humourless in its sentiments. But the next tune taken from the LP was far stronger and fared far better: 'Rock the Casbah', largely written by drummer Topper Headon, hit the Top Ten in the United States, helping propel 'Combat Rock' into the US Top Five. The new medium of MTV certainly helped, putting the video of the song that Don Letts had made on heavy rotation.

In a manner that by now seemed to form a pattern, the Clash chose this moment of glory to shoot themselves in the foot. Even before

Phil Lynott, who cleverly straddled the Old Fart/New Wa
fence, with one version of Kosmo Vinyl.

'Combat Rock' had been released, Topper Headon had been fired from the group, replaced with suitably poetic irony by Terry Chimes, the group's original drummer, libelled on the sleeve of the first LP cover as 'Tory Crimes'. A lengthy world tour followed, including two stints in the United States, where they supported the Who on several stadium dates. By early the next year the Clash had cemented their position as one of the biggest groups in the world. Moreover, their legend as the finest touring and recording rock'n'roll group of all time was firmly in place.

So what better time for the rest of the group to sack one of its most key elements, Mick Jones – who had after all founded the Clash?

The reinstatement of Bernie Rhodes had always been against the better judgement of Jones: the friction that had developed between the two former allies in the latter days of Rhodes' first managerial stint had never evaporated.

When the Clash played the vast US festival in Los Angeles on 28 May 1983, Rhodes intimated to a friend of Jones that the guitarist would not be with the group much longer.

On 10 September the *NME* carried a press release from 'the Clash': 'Joe Strummer and Paul Simonon have decided that Mick Jones should leave the group. It is felt that Jones had drifted away from the original idea of the Clash. In future, it will allow Joe and Paul to get on with the job the Clash set out to do from the beginning.'

'I would like to state that the official press statement is untrue,' responded Mick Jones. 'I would like to make it clear that there was no discussion with Strummer and Simonon prior to my being sacked. I certainly do not feel that I have drifted apart from the original idea of the Clash, and in future I'll be carrying on in the same direction as in the beginning.'

At last the revenge of Bernie Rhodes – always big of mouth and sometimes also of vision, yet forever small in his perverse complexity (why should he have been so fearful of telling inquirers which astrological sign he was born under?) – seemed complete. It was a scenario out of which none of the participants emerged well – especially the entity of the Clash itself.

All the same, a new 'Clash' was formed, bringing in fresh meat guitarists Nick Sheppard and Vince White. The intention was to take the Clash back to basics, performing the group's early material and new similar three- or four-chord songs.

Just to confuse matters Mick Jones teamed up with Topper Headon, announcing that this line-up was the real Clash. But this was little more than a tactic of irritation. Soon Jones devoted himself to the formation of Big Audio Dynamite, linking up with filmmaker Don Letts. For several years they were to have success, blending dance and rock'n'roll music.

Under all manner of pressure – legal, psychic, karmic – the 'dodgy' Clash, as some fans now referred to this line-up, fell apart. They released the 'Cut the Crap' album, which staggered to number sixteen in the UK.

As though all was revealed as to his intentions, the songwriting on 'Cut the Crap' was credited to Strummer-Rhodes. By now, Malcolm McLaren was enjoying his own fifteen minutes of fame as a solo artist; didn't it look as though Rhodes, his close friend and most arch rival, was now also seeking his time in the limelight?

The sexy, sultry weather helped: the temperature never dropped below ninety degrees for the entire stretch of what had been planned as eight dates. Waiting for the group's flight from London on a Monday night at JFK airport, Kosmo Vinyl's chief cause of concern was that the heat was melting the Dixie Peach pomade on his quiff. It seemed churlish to inquire instead as to his feelings about the return of Bernie Rhodes, erstwhile crony in the scam of punk with Malcolm McLaren, to the management helm of the Clash.

Suddenly, in a flurry of hair grease, chrome-encrusted ghetto-blasters, and dramatic shades of pink, ice blue and black, the Clash and their entourage stepped through the arrivals gate into the airport concourse. There was a palpable raising of energy. This could be very good for New York, you felt. This could be a lot of fun. Even the diminutive Rhodes, trailing behind the group in a pair of boat-sized blue suede brothel creepers, had had a facial re-fit: surprisingly, his giant hooter had vanished, and he was blinking from the contact lenses that had replaced his thick-lensed spectacles. That was a lot of fun too.

At the beginning of the year the group had been in temporary disarray. With Vinyl, a former punk in his early twenties, as their business front, the group was managing itself; they had fallen out with the seasoned management team of Peter Jenner and Andrew King in 1980. Strummer, who'd been playing again with his former group the 101'ers, had run into Rhodes in a Wimpy Bar, and arranged a meeting with him and the other Clash members. The deal struck with Rhodes only permitted him a percentage of the group's net profits, so it was in his interests for them to earn wads of cash.

At the core of the group's disquiet were the problems surrounding 'Sandinista', their fourth album. They had had to cut a punitive financial deal before Epic in the USA agreed to a release of the triple-set at the price of a single album. In Britain it was similarly severe: 200,000 copies of 'Sandinista' had to be shifted before the group would receive a penny in royalties - it took years to get there, although the album bettered the sales of 'London Calling' in the States, where it scraped into the Top Twenty.

But after a profitable set of European dates, slotted in when Epic refused tour support for a scheduled sixty-show US tour, the group was firmly back in financial shape. The New York gigs were regarded as the final leg of that tour, which had loosened up the Clash after a year off the road. Bond's was picked after Rhodes and Vinyl visited New York in the early spring. Choosing the tacky former disco as the venue for an eight-night New York stint was in the tradition of the kind of sleazy venues, redolent with low-life romance, into which Rhodes had booked the Clash early in the group's career. Significantly, Rhodes dispensed with the services of an agent, handling the deal himself; this possibly caused problems later. A lot of people in New York were confused by the Bond's dates: the now defunct SoHo News asked me to write a piece investigating why the Clash had turned down Madison Square Garden, where they could have made far more money for far less effort. Find the real story, they said. Here was an abyss-like cultural, even ethical, gap. In the frequent words of members of the group: they didn't understand.

The Clash were staying at the Gramercy Park hotel, located midway between Times Square and Greenwich Village and SoHo. Popular with musicians, the Gramercy was playing host to another group at the same time as the Clash, a fledgling outfit called U2. But, as film crews, graffiti artists, and break-dancers swanning through the lobby made clear, the Gramercy Park had for the

Mick Jones and Paul Simonon with their then main squeezes, Ellen Foley and Pearl Harb

interim quite definitively become Clash Central.

This visit to New York was stage-managed with an efficiency whose machine-like momentum was cleverly concealed; the group's elite status was manipulated for maximum TV and newspaper coverage, in a quantity completely disproportionate to the amount of records the group had so far sold; you'd turn on the TV news and there would be the Clash, paying an official visit to some school in Brooklyn, like alternative statesmen. Two days after the Clash had arrived in New York, on 27 May, a press conference was held at Bond's, in the club's foyer. A journalist pointed out that Paul Weller had accused the Clash of selling out. 'What constitutes a sell-out to the Clash?' he demanded. Mick Jones took up the gauntlet, to toss it to one side. 'What happens,' he said, deadpan, 'is that all the tickets go on sale for a concert, and all the people who want to go go and buy them. And if as many go and buy them as there are tickets, that constitutes a sell-out.' The assembled US media thought this was quite witty.

Manhattan was a perfect backdrop against which to play for a group of former art students in love with the switchblade ethos of Scorsese's Mean Streets. Across the road from Bond's, on 49th Street and Broadway, was a bar in which one of the final scenes of Raging Bull had been shot. The joint, whose mythology included a feminist former bank robber as its manager, was taken over by the Clash posse, who seemed everywhere in New York.

Pearl Harbour, the rockabilly singer, had arrived with Paul Simonon, her boyfriend, to DJ between acts during the shows. Mick Jones was with his then main squeeze Ellen Foley. He threw a splendid birthday party for her at Interferon, the club that a year or so later became Danceteria. Don Letts was making a film about the visit to New York, with a working title of Clash On Broadway – every night after the show he'd been handed a wedge of dollars by Rhodes and told to buy more film. Future members of European royalty could be found snorting coke in cubby-holes at Bond's...Soon new additions to the Clash camp would appear: the graffiti artists Futura 2000 and Fab Five Freddy, for example; even Allen Ginsberg (Allen Ginsberg?). This was the heyday of the New York after-hours bar scene: half dead from tiredness or from what you'd ingested, you'd slide into yet another dubious downtown sleazehole at eight in the morning and find Strummer and Vinyl there, playing pool.

Plus, half the cast of British punk rock seemed to be in New York. John Lydon, busy sneering at everyone, was in residence at some midtown hotel, along with Keith Levine and Jeanette Lee. The Jam had just left. The Fall – Mark E Smith even surpassing Lydon in his sarcasm and certainly in wit – were just about to arrive. At the Peppermint Lounge there was the inevitable latest Johnny Thunders bust benefit.

The temperature had risen yet again, to just over 100 degrees, on the Thursday night the Clash opened at Bond's. In the street outside black kids from Harlem were breakdancing, an early, riveting sighting of a then new phenomenon. Inside the packed hall, though, it was another matter. That night's support act, Grandmaster Flash and the Furious Five, were soundly booed – even pelted with garbage – by this audience of out-of-towners: a logistical whim thrown up by the Ticketron computer ticket sales outlets. (The group seemed amused by the idea of fans travelling to see them, rather than the musicians travelling to the fans. 'It's the mountain coming to Mohammed,' said Strummer.)

Standing halfway down the packed hall with Don Letts, we looked at each other in shocked amazement; it seemed the proof – thereby inducing a comforting sense of self-righteousness – of everything you had heard about the blinkered bigotry of US 'rock' fans. How on earth, you wondered, do they respond to the T-shirt stall in the lobby run by the Committee in Solidarity with the People of El Salvador?

'It's so fucking narrow-minded,' Mick Jones said furiously later. 'I mean, it's an insult to us in a way. We picked the bands to open for us, so supposedly we liked them. They're too narrow-minded to open up to something new.'

But they went crazy for the Clash, in a way I'd never seen a more reserved British audience behave – even truly crackers ones like those at the Glasgow Apollo. And the group seemed lifted by the applause. In the tradition of great rock'n'roll groups, like the Faces and even the Rolling Stones, there had often been something ramshackle, unpredictable, and occasionally shambolic about the Clash's performances. But that was in the past: this group was a powerhouse, tight, tough and immeasurably confident. They played for a long time: two and a half hours or thereabouts. You were struck by their virtuosity, their power, and the variety of material. They kicked off, appropriately , with 'London Calling' and then pillaged all four of their albums for the strongest material. High points were 'Ivan Meets G.I. Joe', 'Career Opportunities', Vince Taylor's 'Brand New Cadillac', and the then new song 'This Is Radio Clash'.

As had happened with their championing of punk, the Clash always had telescopic sights pinned on any coming zeitgeist. Dub reggae, rockabilly, and now rap had been absorbed into their catalogue of material: a mix of 'The Magnificent Seven' was bubbling on black dance stations like KISS, its audiences probably unaware that the Clash were a white, pinko, British guitar group. (Bernie Rhodes was busy wining the likes of influential programme director Frankie Crocker at Harlem soulfood joints.)

But after the set the problems started. Someone had called in the Fire Department and the Manhattan Building Inspector. Bond's had been dangerously oversold; if there had been a fire no more than 900 of the 3,500 strong audience could have escaped; the shows looked about to be cancelled.

A deal was eventually done. The shows could continue if more fire exits were opened up and there was an audience maximum of 1,750. Suddenly the Clash found themselves agreeing to play seventeen dates instead of the eight they'd flown in for. 'I'm very worried about Joe's voice. I hope he can hold up,' pondered Mick Jones. Other members of the group were perhaps greater cause for concern. In an interview sequence filmed by Don Letts, Topper Headon is asked how he feels about having to play a total of seventeen shows. He is unshaven, his voice is slurred, and he is not looking in good shape. It is not a problem, he says, playing all those dates. But his face tells a different story; his face never matches what he is saying. By the time the Clash come back to play New York on the Combat Rock tour, Topper is no longer in the group.

Adversity, however, was turned to advantage. The Friday night show had been cancelled as negotiations dragged on between Rhodes, the club, and the various authorities. As a consequence there was a near riot in Times Square by frustrated ticket-holders: and more TV and press coverage. The additional ten days in New York established the group in the unconscious of the city's cultural underground. Lauded by the likes of Scorsese and De Niro,

137

Before re-joining the Clash Terry Chimes' most recent drumming job had been with Generation X. His debut record with the group had been on the song that was perhaps their best ever record, 'Dancing with Myself'. This tune was later reactivated by Billy Idol when he moved to the United States, reinvented himself, and successfully sold himself as a quintessential British punk: chalk up another unlikely success for MTV-broadcast videos.

as well as kids from Queens with spray-cans, they became a fixture of the coolest edge of the New York art scene. After the dates finally ended they stayed on in the city, to record 'This is Radio Clash'.

Even the support acts began to be given an easier time. Lee 'Scratch' Perry, who the week before had re-painted an entire corridor of the Essex House hotel after he had finished the decor of his bedroom, only baffled the audience.

In the group's dressing-room at Bond's the giant TV was always on. It never worked, just flickering and out of focus. But it was always on. As Scratch painted crosses across one wall, Pearl Harbour negotiated an unsteady path through empty bottles of Remy Martin and crumpled pink plastic carrier bags from Trash and Vaudeville on St Mark's Place, then the retro clothing store in Manhattan and a source of the group's stage-wear. Pearl collapsed into a beat-up armchair; her eyeballs appeared to spin, cartoon-like. Someone had spiked her drink with acid.

Paul Simonon took her to the nearest hospital. As Pearl was wheeled into a casualty, a black hospital orderly walked past them. 'Ring, ring, seven AM,' he rapped with a laugh, hitting them with the first line of 'the Magnificent Seven'.

If anything, that was the proof that the Clash's season at Bond's had worked.

For topping the bill on the New Music Day at the US Festival the Clash were paid half a million US dollars. That was only half of what Van Halen were to receive for headlining on Heavy Metal Day – but Van Halen drew a crowd of 350,000 as opposed to the Clash's 140,000. All the same, just before they were due onstage the group held a press conference at which they announced they would not appear unless the organisers gave an additional $100,000 to disadvantaged children of southern California. In the end, these unfortunates were given somewhere between thirty and forty thousand additional dollars. Why, questioned some, had the Clash not given some of their own money to this clearly heartfelt cause? And why, after being paid so much money, were they two hours late on stage?

Joe Strummer on 'Sandinista': 'We've probably gone in about thirty-six different directions. We've tried things we weren't sure we could do...after a while it became apparent that we were beginning to sit on a pile of tracks. So we thought, let's see how far we can push 'em – CBS that is – as far as price goes. Originally we were intending just to make the usual double, and we weren't bothered about counting the tracks. And then we found it was gonna be a jam fitting it all on a treble, a tight fit.'

Joe Strummer: 'PiL sounds to me like Uriah Heep on mandrax.'

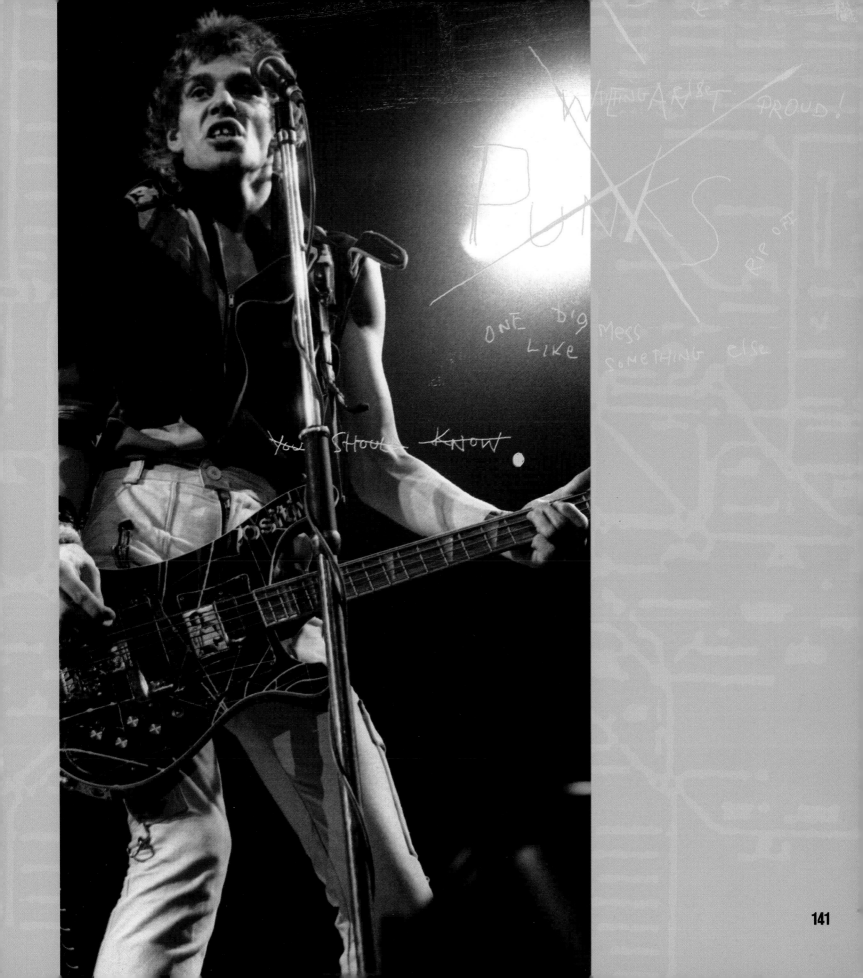

Big Audio Dynamite's video for their 'Medicine Show' single distinguished itself with cameo appearances from several punk luminaries. As well as John Lydon, Joe Strummer and Paul Simonon, the video also featured two former members of the celebrated Rip Rig And Panic - Neneh Cherry and Andrea Oliver: Neneh Cherry was soon to have a successful solo career of her own, whilst Oliver would become a British TV personality in the 1990s.

In April, 1986, Big Audio Dynamite are shooting a video for 'Medicine Show', the second single from the group Mick Jones had formed after being summarily dismissed from the Clash two and a half years previously.

By now, however, a measure of healing has gone on between Jones and Joe Strummer and Paul Simonon. And these two former Clash compadres have been signed up for the shoot, to play uniformed highway patrolmen. Also employed as extras are Neneh Cherry and her longtime companion from Rip Rig and Panic, Andrea Oliver. In just over two years Cherry will be in the charts worldwide with 'Buffalo Stance'; and eight years later Oliver will be co-hosting Britain's Badass TV show with Ice T.

And there is one other extra: John Lydon, aka Johnny Rotten.

When this writer arrives at the video shoot he is having a good day. He has not an ounce of niggling self-doubt. Accordingly, when Mick Jones and Don Letts ask him to go immediately to the 'green room' and 'cool out' John Lydon, he sees no problems with their request.

No-one has told him, however, that Lydon has already consumed about fifteen cans of Red Stripe and probably a ton of sulphate. Or that he has already destroyed a coffee machine worth several hundred pounds.

As soon as he steps into the green room, he can see that things are amiss. Lydon sits on a couch. At the other end of the room is his manager. Wilfully, Lydon drops a cigarette end onto the carpet in front of him. Humiliatingly, his manager is obliged to cross the room to pick it up. Dear me, thinks the writer, John Lydon's been living the life of the cloistered rock'n'roll star in California for too long – not even Led Zeppelin would behave like this.

Top of the Pops, the weekly BBC television round-up of the charts, is playing on the TV set in the green room. Lydon delivers withering attacks on every act that appears.

His criticisms are by no means all correct. And, showing no deference whatsoever to his many frankly puerile comments, the writer picks him up on every point: the guy is talking complete crap.

But no-one has disagreed with this pop star for a long time, it seems. Suddenly, the writer seems to hit a nerve. Without warning, John Lydon stands up in front of him and hits him round the side of the head with a half-full can of Red Stripe. Immediately, the writer leaps up towards him.

But – as though John Lydon now really is a spoiled member of Led Zeppelin – his already humiliated manager leaps to his defence, holding the writer away from him, and removing his client from this already chaotic scene.

Free to roam at will, Lydon disappears onto the set, dangerously firing off an Uzi loaded with blanks next to the ear of the director.

A suitable case for treatment, thinks the writer. Then he thinks something perhaps more valid: what a wanker this man has become.

August, 1986: a curious conjunction of energies brings together the past, the present, and the future of punk music on the set of Straight to Hell, directed by Alex Cox, whose previous film had been Sid and Nancy.

Shot in Almeria in southern Spain, on one of the set locations used by Sergio Leone for his spaghetti westerns, the film stars Joe Strummer, the Pogues, and an unknown 'actress' called Courtney Love.

As she seems a rather sweet girl on set, we are surprised to hear of the reputation Love later arrives at with her group Hole and as wife to Nirvana's Kurt Cobain. Passionately inspired by punk – Cox had come close to casting her as Nancy Spungen for his film – she empathised utterly with Cobain's punk approach in Nirvana.

US bombs flying overhead/There goes my love rocket red

The colour of nighttime neon, the sound of the Terminator
kicking down a metal door, Sigue Sigue Sputnik was Tony
James' rock'n'roll fantasy for the mid-1980s. Unfortunately
it foundered on its ill-advised tag-line of 'designer violence'.

ReSuRRection
Resurrection

10

In the middle of the 1990s something very strange happened in the United States: all of a sudden, it seemed, punk rock became the biggest underground music. Green Day, Rancid and Offspring were at the forefront of this movement, with the first act selling the by now customary music business's yardstick of success of ten million records.

Of course, it wasn't really sudden at all. The group that had established that ten million sales figure had been Nirvana, leaders of the grunge pack, heirs to the spirit of punk. No one more exactly personified America's 'slacker' generation than Kurt Cobain, Nirvana's leader and songwriter.

Like so many of his contemporaries, born in and since the late 1960s, Cobain's dysfunctional family background and daily diet of pop culture and drugs made him both wise and cynical beyond his years: while the trio's music had a narcotic density in which time seemed to be suspended, the fury in Cobain's vocals and lyrics forced out the pain in his soul that drugs are so often used to suppress. As befitted children of their mass-media era, it was not only an underground, snowballing word-of-mouth buzz but also the ceaseless support of the cable and satellite television channel that led to Nirvana's second album, 'Nevermind', released in 1991, selling over ten milion copies.

It is ironic, considering his fondness for the kind of narcotics that regularly bring death to their users that Cobain, fronting Nirvana, was able to kickstart the decomposing corpse of white rock music with a unifying energy that was edifying and elevating. Great rock'n'roll invariably incorporates some form of tribal youth movement; as the spearhead of the Seattle scene, Nirvana became the inspiration for 'grunge', with its recession-friendly thrift shop trappings, a clear reaction against the designer style of the last decade.

As a counterpoint to grunge's hippy-like aura of innocence and honesty, Cobain's public battles with heroin and, it seemed, almost every other available drug, both legal and illegal, became even more celebrated than those of Sid Vicious fifteen or so years previously. One of his inspirations had been a book of photographs of the Sex Pistols. In February, 1992, he married Courtney Love, a singer and sometime actress with a volatile personality whose dresses he would sometimes wear; their apparent love-hate relationship often led to them being described as the Sid and Nancy of grunge. After Cobain and his wife revealed, in a *Vanity Fair* profile, that they had both continued a life of heroin addiction during Love's pregnancy, they seemed mystified at the hostile reader response.

Cobain had been born and brought up in Aberdeen, Washington, a small, isolated logging town a hundred or so miles south of Seattle. His parents divorced when he was eight. Even by then many of the classic errors had been made: a left-handed child, for example, he was forced by his father to be right-handed. The consequences of the official parental split appear to have been disastrous. On his bedroom wall he wrote: 'I hate Mom, I hate Dad, Dad hates Mom, Mom hates Dad, it simply makes you want to be sad.'

In his mid-teens his father, with whom he had been living, re-married and his son moved to his mother's home. In 1984 she learned that her new husband was openly having an affair, and threatened him with one of his own rifles. Then she threw his gun collection into the nearby river. Kurt Cobain observed this from his bedroom window. Later that day he retrieved the guns from the river, sold them and bought his first amplifier.

His father had already given him a guitar when he had turned fourteen. Quickly he had learned to play the chords to 'Louie Louie', as his father knew them; or AC/DC's 'Back in Black' as the tune was identified by his son. Like many American teenagers, he also first began smoking pot at that age; he spent his remaining four high school years permanently stoned. Attempting to 'try to turn my life around' he gave up marijuana for a time and passed an entrance exam to join the navy. Celebrating by smoking his first joint in months he realised that becoming a US sailor was not how he wanted to see his life developing.

Then he sold his Journey and Foreigner albums to raise the money to see Henry Rollins' Black Flag, a

Kurt Cobain: after him, nothing was the same again...

Green Day.

concert that changed Kurt Cobain's life utterly. Instead of going to sea he took a job as a janitor at a local YMCA, where his workmates showed him how to steal prescription drugs, and he developed a fondess for codeine and Vicodin, an opiate-derived painkiller.

In early groups he formed, like Fecal Matter and Brown Towel, his songwriting displayed early signs of the Nirvana sound. 'How successful do you think a band could be if they mixed really heavy Black Sabbath with the Beatles?' Cobain had once pondered. Meeting Chris Novoselic, a bass-player, the pair worked through various drummers (one left to fulfil his ambition of becoming a Burger King manager) before eventually finding Dave Grohl. 'Heavy, light punk rock band: Aerosmith, Led Zeppelin, Black Sabbath, Black Flag, Scratch Acid, Butthole Surfers. Seeks drummer,' ran the copy in a classified advertisement placed by the pair.

In January, 1988, Nirvana, as they had become known, made their first record, at the Seattle studio where Soundgarden had recorded their 'Screaming Life' EP, one of Cobain's favourite records. By now the trio were regularly playing throughout the American north-west. After recording a first album for the Seattle independent label Sub Pop, Nirvana broadened their market, constantly touring the United States, touring Europe for the first time in the autumn of 1989. After reading an interview in which William Burroughs recommended the music of Leadbelly, Cobain developed an obsession with the great American blues singer; his rawness and sincerity struck a chord within him.

Cobain, however, was increasingly plagued with a stomach pain that defied medical diagnosis; on tour he would use drink, drugs or force himself into a catatonic sleeplike state to deaden this mystery ailment. When they first began recording, Cobain's ambition for Nirvana was that everywhere they would attract audiences of 1,000 customers. But through continuous live work, during which they still lived a hand-to-mouth existence, the group began to pass that target.

On 30 April 1991, Nirvana signed with Geffen Records, largely because their heroes Sonic Youth were with the label. On 24 September of that year, 'Nevermind' was released, and Nirvana again set off on tour across the United States. By November 'Nevermind' was in the American Top Ten, and the single 'Teen Spirit' was on heavy rotation on MTV in both America and Europe.

Part of the attraction of Nirvana to their audience was that they seemed distinctly their own men. As their second album sold more and more copies, Cobain began to feel increasingly uncomfortable at becoming part of the music business promotional circus. He would turn down requests for interviews and disdained schmoozing with influential media types. When 'Nevermind' reached number one in America he refused - much to his label's chagrin - to take the group out on another national tour. But this new scarcity only increased interest in Nirvana and sales of the album took a quantum leap.

Emulating Bob Dylan, Cobain had rumours spread that he had been killed in a car crash. Then it was reported that Geffen had turned down the group's third LP, so wilfully had they insisted on recording uncommercial material. But the resulting record, 'In Utero', was another big success. Perhaps more to the point, however, Kurt Cobain had seemed finally to find peace within himself. He insisted that his heroin addiction was over. Even the stomach

Wattie of Scotland's Exploited, Rancid's spiritual antecedents.

Rancid.

pains had ended, he said. Worryingly he soon went into a semi-coma in his Rome hotel, the consequence apparently of a combination of champagne and legal pain-killers. Cobain's rapid recovery, however, suggested this was only a temporary lapse. He returned to his home in Seattle, and on 8 April 1994 was found dead from gunshot wounds.

Dr Feelgood's Lee Brilleaux died of cancer in April 1994, within days of Kurt Cobain. 'One was called a pub rocker and the other a grunge rocker, yet they had punk in common. The two men were, perhaps, scarcely aware of one another, but Brilleaux helped to shape the musical landscape that Cobain came - all too briefly - to inherit,' wrote Paul Du Noyer in *Q*.
     Following hard on the heels of the success of Nirvana was Pearl Jam, another group from Seattle whose LP 'Ten' quickly racked up the statutary ten million sales. When 'Nevermind' had sold over ten million copies, it seemed as though a modern form of punk music finally had taken over the United States, and this seemed only confirmed by the subsequent similar success of Pearl Jam. Challenging the established music business tour booking system, Pearl Jam set up their own value-for-money tours, which only further endorsed their men-of-the-people appeal; it was a stance with which the Clash would heartily have empathised.
     The Clash - as well as politico one-man band Billy Bragg - also seemed at the core of the songs by Green Day, the next set of ten million sellers, with their album 'Dookie'; 'Insomniac' followed in 1995. In fact, it was Green Day who were at the core of the commercial success of US nuevo punk. They became the spokesmen for disaffected teenagers in the USA, paving the way for the almost equally successful, even more alternative Offspring, the most successful act on an independent label in the United States ever - their 'Smash' LP sold six million copies. Without Green Day success would not have come for acts like Rancid, who by the fall of 1995 had sold over half a million albums in the USA, thanks to MTV showing their videos - their Mohican image seems to owe everything to punk acts from the early 1980s like the Exploited, then far too marginal for mass acceptance.

A total transformation of American music seemed to have taken place. In the freneticism of the 90s it had all come together. Twenty years on from 1977, thanks to acts like Green Day, Offspring, and Rancid, the spirit of punk was one of the dominant forces in music as the end of the millennium draws near.

Finally the lunatics had taken over the asylum. Thank God!

Grunge had been the direct artistic descendant of both punks and hippies, continuing the spirit of Johnny Rotten, who was always secretly both. In Seattle grunge and internet culture had converged.

And on 18 March 1996, there took place one of the most extraordinary turnarounds in the entire history of pop music. At the 100 Club in Oxford Street, the scene almost twenty years previously of the Malcolm McLaren punk rock festival, a press conference was held. The cast? The four original members of the Sex Pistols, including Glen Matlock. The subject? The reforming (sic) of the Sex Pistols for a world tour during the summer of 1996.

As though to emphasise the cartoon-like nature of the project, John Lydon had reverted to his original nom-de-disque of Johnny Rotten. Now blonde and bloated ('We love our beer bellies and you will too,' he boasted), with a pineapple haircut that made him look more like a member of Sigue Sigue Sputnik than the Sex Pistols, Rotten-Lydon could all the same display his characteristic scornful wit - which, of course, was lapped up by the media as it had always lapped up everything to do with the Sex Pistols.

The fact that Rotten-Lydon and Glen Matlock would once again be playing together on the same stage drew the most astonishment: in his autobiography Lydon had described feeding the bass-player sandwiches containing Steve Jones' sperm. 'We don't see eye to eye but we have a common interest - your money. It is highly likely that we will just beat the crap out of each other in the first three seconds of the show.'

And he displayed his habitual lack of loyalty to the memory of poor old Sid: 'I was going to put a funeral urn on the table in his place today but unfortunately his ashes were blown all over Heathrow Airport some time ago. I would have needed a Hoover. But this is the original Pistols - Sid was nothing more than a coat hanger to fill an empty space on stage.'

In the June issue of *Q* magazine there was a picture of the Phylossan-era Sex Pistols with Lydon still trying to shock by picking his nose for the camera - as though at forty he had become the Nigel Kennedy of punk rock. Now who were the Boring Old Farts? Did Sid die for this?

In many ways and at various times, thanks to: Joe Strummer, Mick Jones, Paul Simonon, Topper Headon, John Lydon, Paul Cook, Steve Jones, Glen Matlock, Sid Vicious, Bernie Rhodes, Malcolm McLaren, Trish Ronane, Chrissie Hynde, Tony James, Billy Idol, Rat Scabies, Captain Sensible, Jerry Dammers, Jimmy Pursey, Don Letts, Leo Williams, Marc Zermati, Andrea Oliver, Neneh Cherry, Sting, Andy Summers, Stewart Copeland, Jeanette Lee, Gareth Sager, Caroline Coon, Nick Logan, Neil Spencer, Charles Shaar Murray, Danny Baker, Paul Rambali, Mark Ellen, Paul Du Noyer, Vivien Goldman, Kate Simon, Joe Stevens, Lech Kowalski, Timothy White, Jon Savage, Ted and Paul at Rock On, Alan at Out On The Floor, Roger at Ace Records, Andy at Retna, Lennox at Camera Press, Chris, Robert and Mike at Leeds Photovisual (Imaging) Ltd, Clare Hulton, Julian Alexander, Lynne Boot, Pamela Esterson, Versa Manos, Alex Manos, Vicki Fox – for long hours repairing and retouching the hundreds of images used in this book; *MOJO* magazine – in which the section Clash On Broadway originally appeared.

Image research, photo-mechanical and electronic imaging by Exhibit-A. Exhibit-A is the London-based design, archive, and digital image company who, in collaboration with Chris Salewicz, directed and produced both the *Bob Marley: Songs Of Freedom* and *Jimi Hendrix: The Ultimate Experience* books. Exhibit-A is Adrian Boot, Shelley Warren, Vicki Fox and Angela Harrington.

Clearly due to the nature of this subject-matter, many people have said strange and extraordinary things about Punk: wherever possible they, and to whomever they have been speaking, have been credited accordingly. If anyone has been quoted and not credited, it is only because the source could not be found. To anyone so offended, many apologies, serious respect, and deepest thanks.

An Exhibit-A/Chris Salewicz millenium production.

PUNK'S NOT DEAD!!!!!!

Chris Salewicz has documented world popular culture for over two decades, in print, on television and in film. His writing, on subjects from film to foreign affairs, has appeared in *The Sunday Times*, the *Independent*, the *Face*, and countless publications worldwide; crucially for this book he was a senior features writer with *NME* in the second half of the 1970s. He is the author of several books, including – with Adrian Boot – *Bob Marley: Songs Of Freedom* and *Jimi Hendrix: The Ultimate Experience*.

Adrian Boot is one of Britain's most distinguished photographers. His work has appeared regularly in *The Sunday Times*, the *Face*, the *Guardian*, *Rolling Stone*, and countless publications throughout the world. Specialising in photographs taken in developing countries, he was Bob Marley's photographer for many years.

John "Johnny Rotten" Lydon onstage at the Sex Pistols' hugely successful reunion show at London's Finsbury Park in June, 1996